# Knowledge and Learning in Natural Language

'Yang's carefully crafted and impressively argued study is a significant contribution to the exciting field of language acquisition, and cognitive growth more generally. He has shown how conceptions of "universal grammar" can be integrated with precise ideas about learning/growth mechanisms within a variational model of language acquisition that yields sharp and well-confirmed predictions over quite an interesting range, with implications for language change as well. It is a substantial achievement, sure to become the basis for much fruitful inquiry and research.'

Noam Chomsky

'Who would have thought that there could be a synthesis of mathematical learning theory, natural selection and Universal Grammar that is both readable and convincing? Charles Yang has succeeded, and in the process illuminates many phenomena in child language that are perplexing under alternative accounts.'

Jill de Villiers

'Charles Yang attempts to show how the child could acquire both the regular and the irregular verb conjugations using a single mechanism that assigns probability weights to hypotheses on the basis of linguistic evidence from the environment. . . . Yang argues that these irregular patterns are rule-based and that the child's task is not to memorize plurals on a word-by-word basis, but to figure out which rule applies, to which set the noun belongs. If Yang is right, and I think he is, then Pinker's irregulars are not illustrations of the words-and-rules thesis, but the less-general-rules-and-more-general-rules thesis.'

John R. Searle

# Knowledge and Learning in Natural Language

CHARLES D. YANG

# OXFORD
UNIVERSITY PRESS

Great Clarendon Street, Oxford OX2 6DP

Oxford University Press is a department of the University of Oxford.
It furthers the University's objective of excellence in research, scholarship,
and education by publishing worldwide in

Oxford  New York

Auckland  Bangkok  Buenos Aires  Cape Town  Chennai
Dar es Salaam  Delhi  Hong Kong  Istanbul  Karachi  Kolkata
Kuala Lumpur  Madrid  Melbourne  Mexico City  Mumbai  Nairobi
São Paulo  Shanghai  Singapore  Taipei  Tokyo  Toronto

Oxford is a registered trade mark of Oxford University Press
in the UK and in certain other countries

Published in the United States
by Oxford University Press Inc., New York

© Charles Yang 2002

The moral rights of the author have been asserted
Database right Oxford University Press (maker)

First published 2002

All rights reserved. No part of this publication may be reproduced,
stored in a retrieval system, or transmitted, in any form or by any means,
without the prior permission in writing of Oxford University Press,
or as expressly permitted by law, or under terms agreed with the appropriate
reprographics rights organizations. Enquiries concerning reproduction
outside the scope of the above should be sent to the Rights Department,
Oxford University Press, at the address above

You must not circulate this book in any other binding or cover
and you must impose the same condition on any acquirer

British Library Cataloguing in Publication Data

Data available

Library of Congress Cataloging in Publication Data
Yang, Charles D.
Knowledge and learning in natural language/Charles D. Yang.
p. cm.
Includes bibliographical references and index.
1. Language acquisition. 2. Grammar, Comparative and general.
3. Language and languages—Variation. 4. Linguistic change. I. Title
P118.Y36 2002
401'.93—dc21                 2002030758

ISBN 0–19–925414–1
ISBN 0–19–925415–X (pbk.)

1 3 5 7 9 10 8 6 4 2

Typeset in Minion by
Cambrian Typesetters, Frimley, Surrey
Printed in Great Britain
on acid-free paper by
Biddles Ltd., Guildford & King's Lynn

*To my parents and grandma*

# Contents

*Preface*     xi

1 The Study of Language and Language Acquisition     1
    1.1 The naturalistic approach to language     1
    1.2 The structure of language acquisition     4
       1.2.1 Formal sufficiency     5
       1.2.2 Developmental compatibility     6
       1.2.3 Explanatory continuity     9
    1.3 A road map     12

2 A Variational Model of Language Acquisition     14
    2.1 Against transformational learning     15
       2.1.1 Formal insufficiency of the triggering model     18
       2.1.2 Developmental incompatibility of the triggering model     20
       2.1.3 Imperfection in child language?     22
    2.2 The variational approach to language acquisition     24
       2.2.1 The dynamics of Darwinian evolution     24
       2.2.2 Language acquisition as grammar competition     26
    2.3 The dynamics of variational learning     30
       2.3.1 Asymptotic behaviors     30
       2.3.2 Stable multiple grammars     32
       2.3.3 Unambiguous evidence     34
    2.4 Learning grammars in a parametric space     36
       2.4.1 Parameter interference     36
       2.4.2 Independent parameters and signatures     39
       2.4.3 Interference avoidance models     41
       2.4.4 Naive parameter learning     43
       2.4.5 Learning rates and random walks     48
    2.5 Related approaches     53
    Appendix A: Fitness distribution in a three-parameter space     55

3 Rules over Words     59
    3.1 Background     59
    3.2 A model of rule competition     62
       3.2.1 A simple learning task     63
       3.2.2 Rules     64

|  |  | 3.2.3 | Rule competition | 68 |
| | | 3.2.4 | The Absolute and Stochastic Blocking Principles | 73 |
| | 3.3 | Words vs. rules in overregularization | | 75 |
| | | 3.3.1 | The mechanics of the WR model | 75 |
| | | 3.3.2 | The data | 77 |
| | | 3.3.3 | Frequency hierarchy in verb classes | 78 |
| | | 3.3.4 | The free-rider effect | 80 |
| | | 3.3.5 | The effect of phonological regularity: vowel shortening | 82 |
| | 3.4 | Analogy, regularity, and rules | | 83 |
| | | 3.4.1 | The failure of analogy | 83 |
| | | 3.4.2 | Partial regularity and history | 87 |
| | 3.5 | Some purported evidence for the WR model | | 89 |
| | | 3.5.1 | Error rate | 89 |
| | | 3.5.2 | The role of input frequency | 91 |
| | | 3.5.3 | The postulation of the -*d* rule | 92 |
| | | 3.5.4 | Gradual improvement | 93 |
| | | 3.5.5 | Children's judgement | 94 |
| | | 3.5.6 | Anecdotal evidence | 94 |
| | | 3.5.7 | Adult overregularization | 95 |
| | | 3.5.8 | Indecisive verbs | 95 |
| | | 3.5.9 | Irregulars over time | 96 |
| | | 3.5.10 | Corpus statistics | 96 |
| | 3.6 | Conclusion | | 97 |
| | Appendix B: The rule system for English past tense | | | 97 |
| | Appendix C: Overregularization errors in children | | | 98 |
| 4 | Grammar Competition in Children's Syntax | | | 101 |
| | 4.1 | Learning three parameters | | 102 |
| | | 4.1.1 | Verb raising and subject drop: the baselines | 103 |
| | | 4.1.2 | V1 in V2 learners | 105 |
| | 4.2 | Quantifying the stimulus poverty argument | | 109 |
| | 4.3 | The nature of null subjects in children | | 114 |
| | | 4.3.1 | The early acquisition of Chinese and Italian subject drop | 116 |
| | | 4.3.2 | English children speak Chinese | 118 |
| | 4.4 | Summary | | 123 |
| 5 | The Dynamics of Language Change | | | 125 |
| | 5.1 | Grammar competition and language change | | 127 |
| | | 5.1.1 | The role of linguistic evidence | 127 |
| | | 5.1.2 | A variational model of language change | 129 |
| | 5.2 | The loss of V2 in French | | 134 |
| | 5.3 | The erosion of V2 in Middle English | | 138 |
| | | 5.3.1 | Word order in Old English | 138 |
| | | 5.3.2 | The southern dialect | 139 |

|   |   | 5.3.3 The northern dialect and language contact | 141 |
|---|---|---|---|
|   | 5.4 | Limitations of the model | 143 |
| 6 | Summary | | 145 |
|   | 6.1 | Knowledge and learning | 146 |
|   | 6.2 | Principles and variations | 150 |

*References* 153
*Index of Authors* 167
*Subject Index* 171

# Preface

> 'My sons, dig in the vineyard' were the last words of the old man in the fable: and, though the sons found no treasure, they made their fortune by the grapes.
>
> T. H. Huxley

If the heresies in these pages are of any value at all, they result from digging for treasures in a vineyard but harvesting grapes instead. Or, in less romantic terms, the present book started out a pure accident.

In the spring of 1998, I sat in on an excellent class on evolutionary biology with two of the best biologists around: Dick Lewontin and Stephen Jay Gould. There were plenty of treasures but I managed to find some grapes as well. On a field trip to the American Museum of Natural History, while impatiently waiting for SJG for a guided tour, I was struck by a paper that Lewontin wrote in 1983, *Organism as Subject and Object of Evolution*.

Lewontin's paper points out a central feature of evolutionary process that cannot be exaggerated: evolutionary change is a *variational* process. That is, it is not that individuals undergo direct change themselves; rather, it is the distribution of different individuals that changes under evolutionary forces. It immediately occurred to me that language acquisition might be understood in a similar fashion: it is the *distribution* of grammars, not a single grammar itself, that adaptively changes upon exposure to linguistic evidence. Under this view, 'errors' produced by children when learning a language are in fact due to principled grammatical hypotheses attested in other adult languages. The present book, substantially revised from my Ph.D. dissertation at MIT, explores the consequences of this idea.

Of course, knowing where to dig was only a start. In cultivating grapes I have received invaluable advice from my teachers. Noam Chomsky and Bob Berwick are jointly responsible for almost every step in my intellectual development; words of gratitude are not needed for they cannot suffice. Many thanks also to Tom Roeper, for his energy and vast knowledge of child language, and to Patrick Winston, for his good scientific sense and important support during my final days at MIT.

I would like to single out four individuals who have been instrumental to this work. John Frampton and Sam Gutmann made sure my thinking was clear and coherent. Morris Halle taught me everything I know about phonology and devoted an embarrassing amount of time to this work, particularly the chapter on irregular verbs. And finally, Julie Legate read everything I'd ever written and, in many ways, contributed more than anyone else. In addition, I thank her for allowing me to present our joint work in these pages.

Many colleagues and friends examined various parts of the present product at various stages. They are: Steve Anderson, Janet Dean Fodor, Louis Goldstein, Norbert Hornstein, David Lightfoot, Alec Marantz, Fritz Newmeyer, Steven Pinker, Morgan Sonderegger, Jean-Roger Vergnaud, Jill de Villers, Bill Wang, Amy Weinberg, and Ken Wexler. I thank them for encouragement and suggestions. Audiences at many conferences, workshops, and institutions, as well as the students in my seminars at Yale, also helped sharpen some of the ideas developed here. And finally, I am indebted to two anonymous reviewers at Oxford University Press for their good advice on the final manuscript, and John Davey and Jacqueline Smith, my editors, for their patience and support.

This work was funded partially by a graduate fellowship from the National Science Foundation. The Department of Linguistics at Yale provided a warm and supportive environment for the book's completion.

Now, on to the vineyard.

New Haven, Connecticut                                    Charles D. Yang

# 1

# The Study of Language and Language Acquisition

> We may regard language as a natural phenomenon—an aspect of his biological nature, to be studied in the same manner as, for instance, his anatomy.
> Eric H. Lenneberg, *Biological Foundations of Language* (1967), p. vii

## 1.1 The naturalistic approach to language

Fundamental to modern linguistics is the view that human language is a natural object: our species-specific ability to acquire a language, our tacit knowledge of the enormous complexity of language, and our capacity to use language in free, appropriate, and infinite ways are attributed to a property of the natural world, our brain. This position needs no defense, if one considers the study of language is an empirical inquiry.

It follows, then, as in the study of biological sciences, linguistics aims to identify the abstract properties of the biological object under study—human language—and the mechanisms that govern its organization. This has the goal set in the earliest statements on modern linguistics, Chomsky's *The Logical Structure of Linguistic Theory* (1955). Consider the famous duo:

(1) a. Colorless green ideas sleep furiously.
    b. *Furiously sleep ideas green colorless.

Neither sentence has even a remote chance of being encountered in natural discourse, yet every speaker of English can perceive their differences: while they are both meaningless, (1a) is grammatically well formed, whereas (1b) is not. To understand what precisely this difference is is to give 'a rational account of this behavior, i.e., a theory of the speaker's linguistic intuition ... the goal of linguistic theory' (Chomsky 1955/1975: 95)—in other words, a psychology, and ultimately, biology of human language.

Once this position—lately dubbed the *biolinguistic* approach (Jenkins 1999, Chomsky 2000)—is accepted, it follows that language, just like all other biological objects, ought to be studied following the standard methodology in natural sciences (Chomsky 1975, 1980, 1986, 1995a). The postulation of innate linguistic knowledge, the Universal Grammar (UG), is a case in point.

One of the major motivations for innateness of linguistic knowledge comes from the Argument from the Poverty of Stimulus (APS) (Chomsky, 1980: 35). A well-known example concerns the *structure dependency* in language syntax and children's knowledge of it in the absence of learning experience (Chomsky 1975, Crain & Nakayama 1987). Forming an interrogative question in English involves inversion of the auxiliary verb and the subject:

(2) a. Is Alex *e* singing a song?
 b. Has Robin *e* finished reading?

It is important to realize that exposure to such sentences underdetermines the correct operation for question formation. There are many possible hypotheses compatible with the language acquisition data in (2):

(3) a. front the first auxiliary verb in the sentence
 b. front the auxiliary verb that most closely follows a noun
 c. front the last auxiliary verb
 d. front the auxiliary verb whose position in the sentence is a prime number
 e. ...

The correct operation for question formation is, of course, structure-dependent: it involves parsing the sentence into structurally organized phrases, and fronting the auxiliary that follows *the first noun phrase*, which can be arbitrarily long:

(4) a. Is [$_{NP}$ the woman who is sing] *e* happy?
    b. Has [$_{NP}$ the man that is reading a book] *e* had supper?

Hypothesis (3a), which arguably involves simpler mental computation than the correct generalization, yields erroneous predictions:

(5) a. *Is [the woman who *e* singing] is happy?
    b. *Has [the man that *e* finished reading] has finished supper?

But children don't go astray like the creative inductive learner in (3). They stick to the correct operation from very early on, as Crain & Nakayama (1987) showed using elicitation tasks. The children were instructed, 'Ask Jabba if the boy who is watching Mickey Mouse is happy', and no error of the form in (5) was found.

Though sentences like those in (4) may serve to disconfirm hypothesis (3a), they are very rarely if ever encountered by children in normal discourse,[1] not to mention the fact that each of the other incorrect hypotheses in (3) will need to be ruled out by disconfirming evidence. Here lies the logic of the APS:[2] if we know X, and X is underdetermined by learning experience, then X must be innate. The conclusion is then Chomsky's (1975: 33): 'the child's mind ... contains the instruction: Construct a structure-dependent rule, ignoring all structure-independent rules. The principle of structure-dependence is not learned, but forms part of the conditions for language learning.'

The naturalistic approach can also be seen in the evolution of linguistic theories through successive refinement and revision of ideas as their conceptual and empirical flaws are revealed. For example, the 1960s language-particular and construction-specific transformational rules, while descriptively powerful, are inadequate when viewed in a biological context. The complexity and

---

[1] In section 4.2, we will rely on corpus statistics from Legate (1999) and Legate & Yang (in press) to make this remark precise, and to address some recent challenges to the APS by Sampson (1989) and Pullum (1996).

[2] See Crain (1991) for several similar cases, and numerous others in the child language literature.

unrestrictiveness of rules made the acquisition of language wildly difficult: the learner had a vast (and perhaps an infinite) space of hypotheses to entertain. The search for a plausible theory of language acquisition, coupled with comparative linguistic studies, led to the Principles and Parameters (P&P) framework (Chomsky 1981), which suggests that all languages obey a universal (and putatively innate) set of tightly constrained principles, whereas variations across constructions and particular languages—the choices that a child learner has to make during language acquisition—are attributed to a small number of parametric choices.

The present book is a study of language development in children. From a biological perspective, the development of language, like the development of other organic systems, is an interaction between internal and external factors; specifically, between the child's internal knowledge of linguistic structures and the external linguistic experience he receives. Drawing insights from the study of biological evolution, we will put forth a model that make this interaction precise, by embedding a theory of knowledge, the Universal Grammar (UG), into a theory of learning from data. In particular, we propose that language acquisition be modeled as a population of 'grammars', competing to match the external linguistic experiences, much in the manner of natural selection. The justification of this approach will take the naturalistic approach just as in the justification of innate linguistic knowledge: we will provide evidence—conceptual, mathematical, and empirical, and from a number of independent areas of linguistic research, including the acquisition of syntax, the acquisition of phonology, and historical language change—to show that without the postulated model, an adequate explanation of these empirical cases is not possible.

But before we dive into details, some methodological remarks on the study of language acquisition.

## 1.2    The structure of language acquisition

At the most abstract level, language acquisition can be modeled thus:

(6)  $\mathcal{L}: (S_o, E) \rightarrow S_T$

A learning function or algorithm $\mathcal{L}$ maps the initial state of the learner, $S_o$, to the terminal state $S_T$, on the basis of experience $E$ in the environment. Language acquisition research attempts to give an explicit account of this process.

## 1.2.1  Formal sufficiency

The acquisition model must be *causal* and *concrete*. Explanation of language acquisition is not complete with a mere description of child language, no matter how accurate or insightful, without an explicit account of the mechanism responsible for how language develops over time, the learning function $\mathcal{L}$. It is often claimed in the literature that children just 'pick up' their language, or that children's linguistic competence is identical to adults. Such statements, if devoid of a serious effort at some learning-theoretic account of *how* this is achieved, reveal irresponsibility rather than ignorance.

The model must also be *correct*. Given reasonable assumptions about the linguistic data, the duration of learning, the learner's cognitive and computational capacities, and so on, the model must be able to attain the *terminal* state of linguistic knowledge $S_T$ comparable to that of a normal human learner. The correctness of the model must be confirmed by mathematical proof, computer simulation, or other forms of rigorous demonstration. This requirement has traditionally been referred to as the *learnability condition*, which unfortunately carries some misleading connotations. For example, the influential Gold (1967) paradigm of identification in the limit requires that the learner converge onto the 'target' grammar in the linguistic environment. However, this position has little empirical content.[3]

First, language acquisition is the process in which the learner forms an *internalized* knowledge (in his mind), an I-language

---

[3] I am indebted to Noam Chomsky for many discussions on the issue of learnability.

(Chomsky 1986). Language does not exist in the world (in any scientific sense), but resides in the heads of individual users. Hence there is no external target of learning, and hence no 'learnability' in the traditional sense. Second, section 1.2.2 below documents evidence that child language and adult language appear to be sufficiently different that language acquisition cannot be viewed as recapitulation or approximation of the linguistic expressions produced by adults, or of any external target. And third, in order for language to change, the terminal state attained by children must be different from that of their ancestors. This requires that the learnability condition (in the conventional sense) must fail under certain conditions—in particular (as we shall see in Chapter 5) empirical cases where learners do not converge onto any unique 'language' in the informal and E-language sense of 'English' or 'German', but rather a combination of multiple (I-language) grammars. Language change is a result of changes in this kind of grammar combinations.

## 1.2.2  Developmental compatibility

A model of language acquisition is, after all, a model of reality: it must be compatible with what is known about children's language.

Essential to this requirement is the *quantitativeness* of the model. No matter how much innate linguistic knowledge ($S_o$) children are endowed with, language still must be acquired from experience ($E$). And, as we document extensively in this book, not all languages, and not all aspects of a single language, are learned uniformly. As long as this is the case, there remains a possibility that there is something in the input, $E$, that causes such variations. An adequate model of language acquisition must thus consist of an explicit description of the learning mechanisms, $\mathcal{L}$, that quantify the relation between $E$, what the learner receives, and $S_T$, what is acquired. Only then can the respective contribution from $S_o$ and $E$—nature vs. nurture, in a cliché—to language acquisition be understood with any precision.[4]

This urges us to be serious about quantitative comparisons between the input and the attained product of learning: in our case, quantitative measures of child language and those of adult language. Here, many intriguing and revealing disparities surface. A few examples illustrate this observation and the challenge it poses to an acquisition model.

It is now known that some aspects of the grammar are acquired successfully at a remarkably early age. The placement of finite verbs in French matrix clauses is such an example.

(7) Jean voit *souvent/pas* Marie.
Jean sees *often/not* Marie.
'John *often* sees/does *not* see Marie.'

French, in contrast to English, places finite verbs in a position preceding sentential adverbs and negations. Although sentences like (7), indicative of this property of French, are quite rare in adult-to-child speech (7%; estimate based on CHILDES—see MacWhinney & Snow 1985), French children, from as early as can be tested (1;8: Pierce 1989), almost never deviate from the correct form. This discovery has been duplicated in a number of languages with similar properties; see Wexler (1994) and much related work for a survey.

In contrast, some very robustly attested patterns in adult language emerge much later in children. The best-known example is perhaps the phenomenon of subject drop. Children learning English, and other languages that require the presence of a grammatical subject often produce sentences as in (8):

(8) a. (I) help Daddy.
  b. (He) dropped the candy.

Subject drop appears in up to 30% of all sentences around 2;0, and it is not until around 3;0 that they start using subjects at adult

---

[4] This requirement echoes the quantitative approach that has become dominant in theoretical language acquisition over the past two decades—it is no coincidence that the maturation of theoretical linguistics and the construction of large scale child language databases (MacWhinney & Snow 1985) took place around the same time.

level (Valian 1991), in striking contrast to adult language, where subject is used in almost all sentences.

Perhaps more interestingly, children often produce utterances that are virtually absent in adult speech. One such example that has attracted considerable attention is what is known as the Optional Infinitive (OI) stage (e.g. Weverink 1989, Rizzi 1994, Wexler 1994): children acquiring some languages that morphologically express tense nevertheless produce a significant number of sentences where matrix verbs are non-finite. (9) is an example from child Dutch (Weverink 1989):

(9) pappa schoenen wassen
    daddy shoes    to-wash
    'Daddy washes shoes.'

Non-finite root sentences like (9) are ungrammatical in adult Dutch and thus appear very infrequently in acquisition data. Yet OI sentences are robustly used by children for an extended period of time, before they gradually disappear by 2;6 or later.

These quantitative disparities between child and adult language represent a considerable difficulty for empiricist learning models such as neural networks. The problem is, as pointed out by Fodor & Pylyshyn (1988), that learning models without prior knowledge (e.g. UG) can do no more than recapitulate the statistical distribution of the input data. It is therefore unclear how a statistical learning model can duplicate the developmental patterns in child language. That is, during the course of learning,[5]

(10) a. The model must not produce certain patterns that are in principle compatible with the input but never attested (the argument from the poverty of stimulus).
     b. The model must not produce certain patterns abundant in the input (the subject drop phenomenon).
     c. The model must produce certain patterns that are never attested in the input (the Optional Infinitive phenomenon).

---

[5] Note that there is no obvious extralinguistic reason why the early acquisitions are intrinsically 'simpler' to learn than the late acquisitions. For instance, both the obligatory use of subject in English and the placement of finite verbs before/after negation and adverbs involve a binary choice.

Even with the assumption of innate UG, which can be viewed as a kind of prior knowledge from a learning-theoretic perspective, it is not clear how such quantitative disparities can be explained. As will be discussed in Chapter 2, previous formal models of acquisition in the UG tradition in general have not begun to address these questions. The model developed in this study intends to fill this gap.

Finally, quantitative modeling is important to the development of linguistics at large. At the foundation of every 'hard' science is a formal model with which quantitative data can be explained and quantitative predictions can be made and checked. Biology did not come of age until the twin pillars of biological sciences, Mendelian genetics and Darwinian evolution, were successfully integrated into the mathematical theory of population genetics—part of the Modern Synthesis (Mayr & Provine 1980)—where evolutionary change can be explicitly and quantitatively expressed by its internal genetic basis and external environmental conditions.[6] If language development is a biological process, it would certainly be desirable for the interplay between internal linguistic knowledge and external linguistic experience to be quantitatively modeled with formalization.

### 1.2.3  *Explanatory continuity*

Because child language apparently differs from adult language, it is thus essential for an acquisition model to make some choices on explaining such differences. The condition of *explanatory continuity* proposed here imposes some restrictions, or, to be more precise, heuristics, on making these choices.

Explanatory Continuity is an instantiation of the well-known Continuity Hypothesis (Macnamara 1982, Pinker 1984), with roots dating back to Jakobson (1941), Halle (1962), and Chomsky (1965). The Continuity Hypothesis says that, without evidence to

---

[6] See Lewontin (1996) and Maynard Smith (1989) for two particularly insightful introductions to population genetic theories.

the contrary, children's cognitive system is assumed to be identical to that of adults. Since child and adult languages differ, there are two possibilities:

(11) a. Children and adults differ in linguistic performance.
b. Children and adults differ in grammatical competence.

An influential view holds that child competence (e.g. grammar) is identical to adult competence (Pinker 1984). This necessarily leads to a performance-based explanation for child acquisition. There is no question that (11a) is, at some level, true: children are more prone to performance errors than adults, as their memory, processing, and articulation capacities are still underdeveloped. To be sure, adult linguistic performance is affected by these factors as well. However, if and when both approaches are descriptively adequate, there are reasons to prefer competence-based explanations.

Parsimony is the obvious, and primary, reason. By definition, performance involves the interaction between the competence system and other cognitive/perceptual systems. In addition, competence is one of the few components in linguistic performance of which our theoretical understanding has some depth. This is partially because grammatical competence is to a large degree isolated from other cognitive systems—the so-called autonomy of syntax—and is thus more directly accessible to investigation. The tests used for competence studies, often in the form of native speakers' grammatical intuition, can be carefully controlled and evaluated. Finally, and empirically, child language differs from adult language in very specific ways, which do not seem to follow from any general kind of deficit in children's performance.[7] For example, it has been shown that there is much data in child subject drop that does not follow from performance limitation explanations; see e.g. Hyams & Wexler (1993), Roeper & Rohrbacher (1994), Bromberg & Wexler (1995). In Chapter 3, we will show that a theory of English past tense learning based on

---

[7] Obviously, this claim can only be established on a case-by-case basis.

memory lapses (Pinker 1999) fails to explain much of the developmental data reported in Marcus et al. (1992). Phonological rules and structures in irregular verbs must be taken into account to obtain a fuller explanation. And in Chapter 4, we will see additional developmental data from several studies of children's syntax, including the subject drop phenomenon, to show the empirical problems with the performance-based approach.

If we tentatively reject (11a) as, at least, a less favorable research strategy, we must rely on (11b) to explain child language. But exactly how is child competence different from adult competence? Here again are two possibilities:

(12) a. Child competence and adult competence are qualitatively different.
 b. Child competence and adult competence are quantitatively different.

(12a) says that child language is subject to different rules and constraints from adult language. For example, it could be that some linguistic principle operates differently in children from adults, or a piece of grammatical knowledge is absent in younger children but becomes available as a matter of biological maturation (Gleitman 1981, Felix 1987, Borer & Wexler 1987).

It is important to realize that there is nothing unprincipled in postulating a discontinuous competence system to explain child language. If children systematically produce linguistic expressions that defy UG (as understood via adult competence analysis), we can only conclude that their language is governed by different laws. However, in the absence of a concrete theory of how linguistic competence matures (12a) runs the risk of 'anything goes'. It must therefore remain a last resort only when (12b)—the approach that relies on adult competence, for which we do have concrete theories—is shown to be false.[8] More specifically, we must not confuse the difference between child language and *adult*

---

[8] This must be determined for individual problems, although when maturational accounts have been proposed, often non-maturational explanations of the empirical data have not been conclusively ruled out. For example, Borer & Wexler's proposal (1987) that certain A-chains mature have been called into question by many researchers (e.g. Pinker et al. 1987, Demuth 1989, Crain 1991, Allen 1996, Fox & Grodzinsky 1998).

*language* with the difference between child language and *Universal Grammar*. That is, while (part of) child language may not fall under the grammatical system the child eventually attains, it is possible that it falls under some *other*, equally principled grammatical system allowed by UG. (Indeed, this is the approach taken in the present study.)

This leaves us with (12b), which, in combination with (11b), gives the strongest realization of the Continuity Hypothesis: that child language is subject to the same principles and constraints in adult language, and that every utterance in child language is potentially an utterance in adult language. The difference between child and adult languages is due to differences in the *organization* of a continuous grammatical system. This position further splits into two directions:

(13) a. Child language reflects a *unique* potential adult language.
 b. Child language consists of a *collection* of potential adult languages.

(13a), the dominant view ('triggering') in theoretical language acquisition will be rejected in Chapter 2. Our proposal takes the position of (13b): child language in development reflects a statistical combination of possible grammars allowed by UG, only some of which are eventually retained when language acquisition ends. This perspective will be elaborated in the rest of this book, where we examine how it measures up against the criteria of formal sufficiency, developmental compatibility, and explanatory continuity.

## 1.3 A road map

This book is organized as follows.

Chapter 2 first gives a short but critical review of previous approaches to language acquisition. After an encounter with the populational and variational thinking in biological evolution that inspired this work, we propose to model language acquisition as a population of competing grammars, whose distribution changes in response to the linguistic evidence presented to the learner. We will give a precise formulation of this idea, and study its formal/computational properties with respect to the condition of *formal sufficiency*.

Chapter 3 applies the model to one of the biggest developmental problems in language, the learning of English past tense. It will be shown that irregular verbs are organized into classes, each of which is defined by special phonological rules, and that learning an irregular verb involves the competition between the designated special rule and the default *-ed* rule. Again, quantitative predictions are made and checked against children's performance on irregular verbs. Along the way we will develop a critique of Pinker and his colleagues' *Words and Rules* model (Pinker 1999), which holds that irregular verbs are individually and directly memorized as associated pairs of root and past tense forms.

Chapter 4 continues to subject the model to the *developmental compatibility* test by looking at the acquisition of syntax. First, crosslinguistic evidence will be presented to highlight the model's ability to make quantitative predictions based on adult-to-child corpus statistics. In addition, a number of major empirical cases in child language will be examined, including the acquisition of word order in a number of languages, the subject drop phenomenon, and Verb Second.

Chapter 5 extends the acquisition model to the study of language change. The quantitativeness of the acquisition model allows one to view language change as the change in the distribution of grammars in successive generations of learners. This can again incorporate the statistical properties of historical texts in an evolving, dynamic system. We apply the model of language change to explain the loss of Verb Second in Old French and Old English.

Chapter 6 concludes with a discussion on the implications of the acquisition model in a broad context of linguistic and cognitive science research.

# 2

# A Variational Model of Language Acquisition

> One hundred years without Darwin are enough.
> H. J. Muller (1959), on the centennial of *On the Origin of Species*

It is a simple observation that young children's language is different from that of adults. However, this simple observation raises profound questions: What results in the differences between child language and adult language, and how does the child eventually resolve such differences through exposure to linguistic evidence?

These questions are fundamental to language acquisition research. (6) in Chapter 1, repeated below as (14), provides a useful framework within to characterize approaches to language acquisition:

(14)   $\mathcal{L}: (S_o, E) \to S_T$

Language acquisition can be viewed as a function or algorithm, $\mathcal{L}$, which maps the initial and hence putatively innate state ($S_o$) of the learner to the terminal state ($S_T$), the adult-form language, on the basis of experience, $E$, in the environment.

Two leading approaches to $\mathcal{L}$ can be distinguished in this formulation according to the degree of focus on $S_o$ and $\mathcal{L}$. An empiricist approach minimizes the role of $S_o$, the learner's initial (innate) and domain-specific knowledge of natural language. Rather, emphasis is given to $\mathcal{L}$, which is claimed to be a generalized learning mechanism cross-cutting cognitive domains. Models in this approach can broadly be labeled *generalized statistical learning* (GSL): learning is the approximation of the terminal state ($S_T$)

based on the statistical distribution of the input data. In contrast, a rationalist approach, often rooted in the tradition of generative grammar, attributes the success of language acquisition to a richly endowed $S_0$, while relegating $L$ to a background role. Specifically, $S_0$ is assumed to be a delimited space, a Universal Grammar (UG), which consists of a finite number of hypotheses that a child can in principle entertain. Almost all theories of acquisition in the UG-based approach can called *transformational learning* models, borrowing a term from evolutionary biology (Lewontin 1983): the learner's linguistic hypothesis undergoes direct transformations (changes), by moving from one hypothesis to another, driven by linguistic evidence.

This study introduces a new approach to language acquisition in which both $S_0$ and $L$ are given prominent roles in explaining child language. We will show that once the domain-specific and innate knowledge of language ($S_0$) is assumed, the mechanism language acquisition ($L$) can be related harmoniously to the learning theories from traditional psychology, and possibly, the development of neural systems.

## 2.1 Against transformational learning

Recall from Chapter 1 the three conditions on an adequate acquisition model:

(15)   a.  formal sufficiency
        b.  developmental compatibility
        c.  explanatory continuity

If one accepts these as guidelines for acquisition research, we can put the empiricist GSL models and the UG-based transformational learning models to the test.

In recent years, the GSL approach to language acquisition has (re)gained popularity in cognitive sciences and computational linguistics (see e.g. Bates & Elman 1996, Seidenberg 1997). The GSL approach claims to assume little about the learner's initial knowledge of language. The child learner is viewed as a generalized data processor, such as an artificial neural network, which approximates the adult language based on the statistical distribution of the input data. The GSL approach claims support (Bates & Elman 1996) from experiments showing that infants are capable of extracting statistical regularities in (quasi)linguistic information (e.g. Saffran et al. 1996).

Despite this renewed enthusiasm, it is regrettable that the GSL approach has not tackled the problem of language acquisition in a broad empirical context. For example, a main line of work (e.g. Elman 1990, 1991) is dedicated to showing that certain neural network models are able to capture some limited aspects of syntactic structures—a most rudimentary form of the formal sufficiency condition—although there is still debate on whether this project has been successful (e.g. Marcus 1998). Much more effort has gone into the learning of irregular verbs, starting with Rumelhart & McClelland (1986) and followed by numerous others,[1] which prompted a review of the connectionist manifesto, *Rethinking Innateness* (Elman et al. 1996), to remark that connectionist modeling makes one feel as if developmental psycholinguistics is only about 'development of the lexicon and past tense verb morphology'(Rispoli 1999: 220). But even for such a trivial problem, no connectionist network has passed the *Wug*-test (Prasada & Pinker 1993, Pinker 1999), and, as we shall see in Chapter 3, much of the complexity in past tense acquisition is not covered by these works.

As suggested in section 1.2.2, there is reason to believe that these challenges are formidable for generalized learning models such as an artificial neural network. Given the power of computational tools available today, it would not be remarkable to construct a (GSL) system that learns something. What *would* be remarkable is to discover whether the constructed system learns in much the same way that human children learn. (10) shows that child language and adult language display significant disparities in statistical distributions; what the GSL approach has to do, then, is

---

[1] Pinker (1999: 302) lists 25 major connectionist studies on irregular verbs.

to find an empiricist (learning-theoretic) alternative to the learning biases introduced by innate UG. This seems difficult, given the simultaneous constraints—from both child language acquisition and comparative studies of the world's languages—that such an alternative must satisfy. That is, an empiricist must account for, say, systematic utterances like *me riding horse* (meaning 'I am riding a horse') in child language and island constraints in adult language, at the same time. But again, nothing can be said unless the GSL approach faces the challenges from the quantitative and crosslinguistic study of child language; as pointed out by Lightfoot (1998), Fodor & Crowther (in press), and others, there is nothing on offer.

We thus focus our attention on the other leading approach to language acquisition, which is most closely associated with generative linguistics. We will not review the argument for innate linguistic knowledge; see section 1.1 for a simple yet convincing example. The restrictiveness in the child language learner's hypothesis space, coupled with the similarities revealed in comparative studies of the world's languages, have led linguists to conclude that human languages are delimited in a finite space of possibilities, the Universal Grammar. The Principles and Parameters (P&P) approach (Chomsky 1981) is an influential instantiation of this idea by attempting to constrain the space of linguistic variation to a set of parametric choices.

In generative linguistics, the dominant model of language acquisition (e.g. Chomsky 1965, Wexler & Culicover 1980, Berwick 1985, Hyams 1986, Dresher & Kaye 1990, Gibson & Wexler 1994) can be called the *transformational learning* (TL) approach. It assumes that the state of the learner undergoes direct changes, as the old hypothesis is replaced by a new hypothesis. In the *Aspects*-style framework (Chomsky 1965), it is assumed (Wexler & Culicover 1980, Berwick 1985) that when presented with a sentence that the learner is unable to analyze with the present set of rules, an appropriate rule is added to the current hypothesis. Hence, a new hypothesis is formed to replace the old. With the advent of the P&P framework, acquiring a language has been viewed as setting the appropriate parameters. An influential way to implement parameter setting is the *triggering* model (Chomsky 1981, Gibson & Wexler 1994). In a typical triggering algorithm, the learner changes the value of a parameter in the present grammar if the present grammar cannot analyze an incoming sentence and the grammar with the changed parameter value can. Again, a new hypothesis replaces the old hypothesis. Note that in all TL models, the learner changes hypotheses in an all-or-nothing manner; specifically for the triggering model, the UG-defined parameters are literally 'triggered' (switched on and off) by the relevant evidence. For the rest of our discussion, we will focus on the triggering model (Gibson & Wexler 1994), representative of the TL models in the UG-based approach to language acquisition.

### 2.1.1 Formal insufficiency of the triggering model

It is by now well known that Gibson & Wexler's triggering model has a number of formal problems (see Berwick & Niyogi 1996, Frank & Kapur 1996, Dresher 1999). The first problem concerns the existence of local maxima in the learning space. Local maxima are non-target grammars from which the learner can never reach the target grammar.[2] By analyzing the triggering model as a Markovian process in a finite space of grammars, Berwick & Niyogi (1996) have demonstrated the pervasiveness of local maxima in Gibson and Wexler's (very small) three-parameter space. Gibson & Wexler (1994) suggest that the local maxima problem might be circumvented if the learner starts from a default parameter setting, a 'safe' state, such that no local maximum can ever be encountered. However, Kohl (1999), using an exhaustive search in a computer implementation of the triggering model, shows that in a linguistically realistic twelve-parameter space, 2,336 of the 4,096 grammars are still not learnable even

---

[2] The present discussion concerns acquisition in a *homogeneous* environment in which all input data can be identified with a single, idealized 'grammar'. For historical reasons we continue to refer to it by the traditional term 'target grammar'.

with the best default starting state. With the worst starting state, 3,892 grammars are unlearnable. Overall, there are on average 3,348 unlearnable grammars for the triggering model.[3]

A second and related problem has to do with the ambiguity of input evidence. In a broad sense, ambiguous evidence refers to sentences that are compatible with more than one grammar. For example, a sentence with an overt thematic subject is ambiguous between an English-type grammar, which obligatorily uses subjects, and a Chinese-type grammar, which optionally uses subjects. When ambiguous evidence is presented, it may select any of the grammars compatible with the evidence and may subsequently be led to local maxima and unlearnability. To resolve the ambiguity problem, Fodor's (1998) Structural Trigger Learner (STL) model assumes that the learner can determine whether an input sentence is unambiguous by attempting to analyze it with multiple grammars. Only evidence that unambiguously determines the target grammar triggers the learner to change parameter values. Although Fodor shows that there is unambiguous evidence for each of the eight grammars in Gibson & Wexler's three-parameter space, such optimistic expectations may not hold for a large parametric space in general (Clark 1992, Clark & Roberts 1993; we return to this with a concrete example in section 2.3.3). Without unambiguous evidence, Fodor's revised triggering model will not work.

Lastly, the robustness of the triggering model has been called into question. As pointed out by Osherson et al. (1984), Randall (1990), and Valian (1990), even a small amount of noise can lead the triggering-like transformational models to converge on a wrong grammar. In a most extreme form, if the *last* sentence the

---

[3] Niyogi & Berwick (1995) argue that 'mis-convergence', i.e. the learner attaining a grammar that is different from target grammar, is what makes language change possible: hence formal insufficiency of the triggering model may be a virtue instead of a defect. However, empirical facts from diachronic studies suggest a different picture of how language changes; see Ch. 5. In addition, whatever positive implications of misconvergence are surely negated by the overwhelming failure to converge, as Kohl's results show.

learner hears just before language acquisition stops happens to be noise, the learning experience during the entire period of language acquisition is wasted. This scenario is by no means an exaggeration when a realistic learning environment is taken into account. Actual linguistic environments are hardly uniform with respect to a single idealized grammar. For example, Weinreich et al. (1968: 101) observe that it is unrealistic to study language as a 'homogeneous object', and that the 'nativelike command of heterogeneous structures is not a matter of multidialectalism or "mere" performance, but is part of unilingual linguistic competence'. To take a concrete example, consider again the acquisition of subject use. English speakers, who in general use overt subjects, do occasionally omit them in informal speech, e.g. *Seems good to me*. This pattern, of course, is compatible with an optional subject grammar. Now recall that a triggering learner can alter its hypothesis on the basic of a *single* sentence. Consequently, variability in linguistic evidence, however sparse, may still lead a triggering learner to swing back and forth between grammars like a pendulum.

## 2.1.2  Developmental incompatibility of the triggering model

While it might be possible to salvage the triggering model to meet the formal sufficiency condition (e.g. via a random-walk algorithm of Niyogi & Berwick 1996; but cf. Sakas & Fodor 2001), the difficulty posed by the developmental compatibility condition is far more serious. In the triggering model, and in fact in *all* TL models, the learner at any one time is identified with a single grammar. If such models are at all relevant to the explanation of child language, the following predictions are inevitable:

(16) a. The learner's linguistic production ought to be consistent with respect to the grammar that is currently assumed.
 b. As the learner moves from grammar to grammar, abrupt changes in linguistic expressions should be observed.

To the best of my knowledge, there is in general no developmental evidence in support of either (16a) or (16b).

A good test case is again children's null subjects (NS), where we have a large body of quantitative and crosslinguistic data. First, consider the prediction in (16a), the consistency of child language with respect to a single grammar defined in the UG space. Working in the P&P framework, Hyams (1986), in her groundbreaking work, suggests that English child NS results from mis-setting their language to an optional-subject grammar such as Italian, in which subject drop is grammatical. However, Valian (1991) shows that while Italian children drop subjects in 70% of all sentences, the NS ratio is only 31% for American children in the same age group. This statistical difference renders it unlikely that English children initially use an Italian-type grammar. Alternatively, Hyams (1991) suggests that during the NS stage, English children use a discourse-based, optional-subject grammar like Chinese. However, Wang et al. (1992) show that while subject drop rate is only 26% for American children during the NS stage (2;0–3;0),[4] Chinese children in the same age group drop subjects in 55% of all sentences. Furthermore, if English children did indeed use a Chinese-type grammar, one predicts that object drop, grammatical in Chinese, should also be robustly attested (see section 4.3.2 for additional discussion). This is again incorrect: Wang et al. (1992) find that for 2-year-olds, Chinese children drop objects in 20% of sentences containing objects and American children only 8%. These comparative studies conclusively demonstrate that subject drop in child English cannot be identified with any single adult grammar.

Turning now to the triggering models' second prediction for language development (16b), we expect to observe abrupt changes

---

[4] This figure, as well as Valian's (1991), is lower than those reported elsewhere in the literature, e.g. Bloom (1993), Hyams & Wexler (1993). However, there is good reason to believe that around 30% is a more accurate estimate of children's NS rate. In particular, Wang et al. (1992) excluded children's NS sentences such as infinitives and gerunds that would be acceptable in adult English; see Phillips (1995) for an extended discussion on the counting procedure.

in child language as the learner switches from one grammar to another. However, Bloom (1993) found no sharp changes in the frequency of subject use throughout the NS stage of Adam and Eve, two American children studied by Brown (1973). Behrens (1993) reports similar findings in a large longitudinal study of German children's NS stage. Hence, there is no evidence for a radical reorganization—parameter resetting (Hyams & Wexler 1993)—of the learner's grammar. In section 4.1 we will show that for Dutch acquisition, the percentage of V2 use in matrix sentences also rises gradually, from about 50% at 2;4 to 85% at 3;0. Again, there is no indication of a radical change in the child's grammar, contrary to what the triggering model entails. Overall, the gradualness of language development is unexpected in the view of all-or-none parameter setting, and has been a major argument against the parameter-setting model of language acquisition (Valian 1990, 1991, Bloom 1990, 1993), forcing many researchers to the conclusion that child and adult language differ not in competence but in performance.

## 2.1.3 Imperfection in child language?

So the challenge remains: what explains the differences between child and adult languages? As summarized in Chapter 1 and repeated below, two approaches have been advanced to account for the differences between child and adult languages:

(17) a. Children and adults differ in linguistic performance.
 b. Children and adults differ in grammatical competence.

The performance deficit approach (17a) is often stated under the Continuity Hypothesis (Macnamara 1982, Pinker 1984). It assumes an identity relation between child and adult competence, while attributing differences between child and adult linguistic forms to performance factors inherent in production, and (nonlinguistic) perceptual and cognitive capacities that are still underdeveloped at a young age (e.g. Pinker 1984, Bloom 1990, 1993, Gerken 1991, Valian 1991).

The competence deficit approach (17b) is more often found in works in the parameter-setting framework. In recent years it has been claimed (Hyams 1996, Wexler 1998), in contrast to earlier ideas of parameter mis-setting, that the parameter values are set correctly by children very early on.[5] The differences between child language and adult language have been attributed to other deficits in children's grammatical competence. For example, one influential approach to the OI phenomenon reviewed in section 1.2.2 assumes a deficit in the Tense/Agreement node in children's syntactic representation (Wexler 1994): the Tense/Agreement features are missing in young children during the ROI stage. Another influential proposal in Rizzi's (1994) *Truncation Hypothesis* holds that certain projections in the syntactic representation, specifically CP, are missing in young children's knowledge of language. The reader is referred to Phillips (1995) for a review and critique of some recent proposals along these lines.

Despite the differences between the two approaches, a common theme can be identified: child language is assumed to be an *imperfect* form of adult language, perturbed by either competence or performance factors. In section 1.2.3, we have already noted some methodological pitfalls associated with such explanatorily discontinuous accounts. More empirically, as we shall see in Chapters 3 and 4, the imperfection perspective on child language leaves many developmental patterns unexplained. To give a quick preview, we will see that children's over-regularization errors (*hold-holded*) reveal important clues on how phonology is structured and learned, and should not be regarded as simple memory retrieval failures as in Pinker (1999). We will see that when English children drop subjects in *Wh* questions, they do so almost always in adjunct (*where, how*) questions, but almost never in argument (*who, what*) questions: a categorical asymmetry not predicted by any imperfection explanation proposed so far. We will document the robust use

---

[5] Although it is not clear how parameters are set (correctly), given the formal insufficiency of the triggering model reviewed earlier.

(approximately 50%) of V1 patterns in children acquiring V2: hence, 50% of 'imperfection' to be explained away.

This concludes our very brief review of the leading approaches to language acquisition. While there is no doubt that innate UG knowledge must play a crucial role in constraining the child's hypothesis space and the learning process, there is *one* component in the GSL approach that is too sensible to dismiss. That is, statistical learning seems most naturally suited to modeling the gradualness of language development. In the rest of this chapter we propose a new approach that incorporates this useful aspect of the GSL model into a generative framework: an innate UG provides the *hypothesis space* and statistical learning provides the *mechanism*. To do this, we draw inspiration from Darwinian evolutionary biology.

## 2.2 The variational approach to language acquisition

### 2.2.1 *The dynamics of Darwinian evolution*

We started the discussion of child language by noting the variation between child and adult languages. It is a fundamental question how such variation is interpreted in a theory of language acquisition. Here, the conceptual foundation of Darwinian evolutionary thinking provides an informative lesson.

Variation, as an intrinsic fact of life, can be observed at many levels of biological organizations, often manifested in physiological, developmental, and ecological characteristics. However, variation among individuals in a population was not fully recognized until Darwin's day. As pointed out by Ernst Mayr on many occasions (in particular, 1963, 1982, 1993), it was Darwin who first realized that the variations among individuals are 'real': individuals in a population are inherently different, and are not mere 'imperfect' deviations from some idealized archetype.

Once the reality of variation and the uniqueness of individuals were recognized, the correct conception of evolution became possible: variations at the individual level result in fitness variations at the population level, thus allowing evolutionary forces such as natural selection to operate. As R. C. Lewontin remarks, evolutionary changes are hence changes in the *distribution* of different individuals in the population:

> Before Darwin, theories of historical change were all *transformational*. That is, systems were seen as undergoing change in time because each element in the system underwent an individual transformation during its history. Lamarck's theory of evolution was transformational in regarding species as changing because each individual organism within the species underwent the same change. Through inner will and striving, an organism would change its nature, and that change in nature would be transmitted to its offspring.
>
> In contrast, Darwin proposed a *variational* principle, that individual members of the ensemble differ from each other in some properties and that the system evolves by changes in the proportions of the different types. There is a sorting-out process in which some variant types persist while others disappear, so the nature of the ensemble as a whole changes without any successive changes in the individual members. (Lewontin 1983: 65–6; italics original.)

For scientific observations, the message embedded in Darwinian variational thinking is profound. Non-uniformity in a sample of data often should, as in evolution, be interpreted as a collection of *distinct* individuals: variations are therefore real and expected, and should not be viewed as 'imperfect' forms of a single archetype. In the case of language acquisition, the differences between child and adult languages may not be the child's imperfect grasp of adult language; rather, they may actually reflect a principled grammatical system in development and transition, before the terminal state is established. Similarly, the distinction between transformational and variational thinking in evolutionary biology is also instructive for constructing a formal model of language acquisition. Transformational learning models identify the learner with a single hypothesis, which directly changes as input is processed. In contrast, we may consider a variational theory in which language acquisition is the change in the *distribution* of I-language grammars, the principled variations in human language.

In what follows, we present a learning model that instantiates the variational approach to language acquisition. The computational properties of the model will then be discussed in the context of the formal sufficiency condition on acquisition theories.

### 2.2.2 Language acquisition as grammar competition

To explain the non-uniformity and the gradualness in child language, we explicitly introduce statistical notions into our learning model. We adopt the P&P framework, i.e. assuming that there is only a finite number of possible human grammars, varying along some parametric dimensions. We also adopt the strongest version of continuity hypothesis, which says, without evidence to the contrary, that UG-defined grammars are accessible to the learner from the start.

Each grammar $G_i$ is paired with a weight $p_i$, which can be viewed as the measure of prominence of $G_i$ in the learner's language faculty. In a linguistic environment $E$, the weight $p_i(E, t)$ is determined by the learning function $\mathcal{L}$, the linguistic evidence in $E$, and the time variable $t$, the time since the outset of language acquisition. Learning stops when the weights of all grammars are stabilized and do not change any further,[6] possibly corresponding to some kind of critical period of development. In particular, in an idealized environment where *all* linguistic expressions are generated by a 'target' grammar $T$—again, keeping to the traditional terminology—we say that learning *converges to target* if $p_T = 1$ when learning stops. That is, the target grammar has eliminated all other grammars in the population as a result of learning.

The learning model is schematically shown below:

(18) Upon the presentation of an input datum $s$, the child
 a. selects a grammar $G_i$ with the probability $p_i$
 b. analyzes $s$ with $G_i$

---

[6] This does not mean that learning necessarily converges to a single grammar; see (24) below.

c. 
- if successful, reward $G_i$ by increasing $p_i$
- otherwise, punish $G_i$ by decreasing $p_i$

Metaphorically speaking, the learning hypotheses—the grammars defined by UG—*compete*: grammars that succeed in analyzing a sentence are rewarded and those that fail are punished. As learning proceeds, grammars that have overall more success with the data will be more prominently represented in the learner's hypothesis space.

An example illustrates how the model works. Imagine the learner has two grammars, $G_1$, the target grammar used in the environment, and $G_2$, the competitor, with associated weights of $p_1$ and $p_2$ respectively. Initially, the two grammars are undifferentiated, i.e. with comparable weights. The learner will then have comparable probabilities of selecting the grammars for both input analysis and sentence production, following the null hypothesis that there is a single grammatical system responsible for both comprehension/learning and production. At this time, sentence sequences produced by the learner will look like this:

(19) Early in acquisition:
$S_{G1}, S_{G1}, S_{G2}, S_{G1}, S_{G2}, S_{G2}, \ldots$

where $S_G$ indicates a sentence produced by the grammar $G$.[7]

As learning proceeds, $G_2$, which by assumption is incompatible with at least *some* input data, will be punished and its weight will gradually decrease. At this stage of acquisition, sequences produced by the learner will look like this:

(20) Intermediate in acquisition:
$S_{G1}, S_{G1}, S_{G2}, S_{G1}, S_{G1}, S_{G1} \ldots$

where $G_1$ will be more and more dominantly represented.

When learning stops, $G_2$ will have been eliminated ($p_2 \approx 0$) and $G_1$ is the only grammar the learner has access to:

(21) Completion of acquisition:
$S_{G1}, S_{G1}, S_{G1}, S_{G1}, S_{G1}, S_{G1}, \ldots$

---

[7] It is possible that some sentences are ambiguous between $G_1$ and $G_2$, which may extensionally overlap.

Of course, grammars do not actually compete with each other: the competition metaphor only serves to illustrate (a) the grammars' coexistence and (b) their differential representation in the learner's language faculty. Neither does the learner play God by supervising the competition of the grammars and selecting the winners.[8] We will also stress the *passiveness* of the learner in the learning process, conforming to the research strategy of a 'dumb' learner in language acquisition. That is, one does not want to endow the learner with too much computational power or too much of an active role in learning. The justification for this minimum assumption is twofold. On the one hand, successful language acquisition is possible, barring pathological cases, irrespective of 'general intelligence'; on the other, we simply don't have a theory of children's cognitive/computational capacities to put into a rigorous model of acquisition—an argument from ignorance. Hence, we assume that the learner does not contemplate which grammar to use when an input datum is presented. He uses whichever happens to be selected with its associated weight/probability. He does not make active changes to the selected grammar (as in the triggering model), or reorganize his grammar space, but simply updates the weight of the grammar selected and moves on.

Some notations. Write $s \in E$ if a sentence $s$ is an utterance in the linguistic environment $E$. We assume that during the time frame of language acquisition, $E$ is a fixed environment, from which $s$ is drawn independently. Write $G \to s$ if a grammar $G$ can analyze $s$, which, as a special case, can be interpreted as parsability (Wexler & Culicover 1980, Berwick 1985), in the sense of *strong generative capacity*. Clearly, the weak generative notion of string-grammar acceptance does not affect formal properties of the model. However, as we shall see in Chapter 4, children use their morphological knowledge and domain-specific knowledge of UG—strong

---

[8] In this respect, the variational model differs from a similar model of acquisition (Clark 1992), in which the learner is viewed as a genetic algorithm that explicitly evaluates grammar fitness. We return to this in section 2.5.

generative notions—to disambiguate grammars. It is worth noting that the formal properties of the model are independent of the definition of analyzability: any well-defined and empirically justified notion will suffice. Our choice of string-grammar compatibility obviously eases the evaluation of grammars using linguistic corpora.

Suppose that there are altogether $N$ grammars in the population. For simplicity, write $p_i$ for $p_i(E, t)$ at time $t$, and $p_i'$ for $p_i(E, t+1)$ at time $t+1$. Each time instance denotes the presentation of an input sentence. In the present model, learning is the adaptive change in the weights of grammars in response to the sentences successively presented to the learner. There are many possible instantiations of competition-based learning.[9] Consider the one in (22):

(22) Given an input sentence $s$, the learner selects a grammar $G_i$ with probability $p_i$:

a. if $G_i \to s$ then $\begin{cases} p_i' = p_i + \gamma(1 - p_i) \\ p_j' = (1 - \gamma)p_j & \text{if } j \neq i \end{cases}$

b. if $G_i \not\to s$ then $\begin{cases} p_i' = (1 - \gamma)p_i \\ p_j' = \dfrac{\gamma}{N-1} + (1 - \gamma)p_j & \text{if } j \neq i \end{cases}$

(22) is the Linear reward-penalty ($L_{R-P}$) scheme (Bush & Mosteller 1951, 1958), one of the earliest, simplest, and most extensively studied learning models in mathematical psychology. Many similar competition-based models have been formally and experimentally studied, and receive considerable support from human and and animal learning and decision-making; see Atkinson et al. (1965) for a review.

Does the employment of a general-purpose learning model from the behaviorist tradition, the $L_{R-P}$, signal a return to the Dark Ages? Absolutely not. In competition learning models, what is crucial is the constitution of the hypothesis space. In the original $L_{R-P}$ scheme, the hypothesis space consists of simple responses

---

[9] See Yang & Gutmann (1999) for a model that uses a Hebbian style of update rules.

conditioned on external stimulus; in the grammar competition model, the hypothesis space consists of Universal Grammar, a highly constrained and finite range of possibilities. In addition, as discussed in Chapter 1, it seems unlikely that language acquisition can be equated to data-driven learning without prior knowledge. And, as will be discussed in later chapters in addition to numerous other studies in language acquisition, in order adequately to account for child language development, one needs to make reference to specific characterization of UG supplied by linguistic theories.

There is yet another reason for having an explicit account of the learning process: because language *is* acquired, and thus the composition, distribution, and other properties of the input evidence, in principle, matter. The landmark study of Newport et al. (1977) is best remembered for debunking the necessity of the so-called 'Motherese' for language acquisition, but it also shows that the development of *some* aspects of language does correlate with the abundance of linguistic data. Specifically, children who are exposed to more yes/no questions tend to use auxiliary verbs faster and better. An explicit model of learning that incorporates the role of input evidence may tell us why such correlations exist in some cases, but not others (e.g. the null subject phenomenon). The reason, as we shall see, lies in the Universal Grammar.

Hence, our emphasis on $\mathcal{L}$ is simply a plea to pay attention to the actual mechanism of language development, and a concrete proposal of what it might be.

## 2.3 The dynamics of variational learning

We now turn to the computational properties of the variational model in (22).

### 2.3.1 *Asymptotic behaviors*

In any competition process, some measure of fitness is required. Adapting the formulation of Bush & Mosteller (1958), we may offer the following definition:

(23) The *penalty probability* of grammar $G_i$ in a linguistic environment $E$ is

$$c_i = \Pr(G_i \not\to s \mid s \in E)$$

The penalty probability $c_i$ represents the probability that a grammar $G_i$ fails to analyze an incoming sentence and gets punished as a result. In other words, $c_i$ is the percentage of sentences in the environment with which the grammar $G_i$ is incompatible. Notice that penalty probability is a fixed property of a grammar relative to a fixed linguistic environment $E$, from which input sentences are drawn.

For example, consider a Germanic V2 environment, where the main verb is situated in the second constituent position. A V2 grammar, of course, has the penalty probability of 0.[10] An English-type SVO grammar, although not compatible with all V2 sentences, is nevertheless compatible with a certain proportion of them. According to a corpus analysis cited in Lightfoot (1997), about 70% of matrix sentences in modern V2 languages have the surface order of SVO: an SVO grammar therefore has a penalty probability of 30% in a V2 environment. Since the grammars in the delimited UG space are fixed—it is only their weights that change during learning—their fitness values defined as penalty probabilities are also fixed if the linguistic environment is, by assumption, fixed.

It is crucial to realize that penalty probability is an *extensionally* defined property of grammars. It is a notion used, by the linguist, in the formal analysis of the learning model. It is not a component of the learning process. For example, the learner needs not and does not keep track of frequency information about sentence patterns, and does not explicitly compute the penalty probabilities of the competing grammars. Nor is penalty probability represented or accessed in during learning, as the model in (22) makes clear.

---

[10] For expository ease we will keep to the fitness measure of whole grammars in the present discussion. In section 2.4 we will place the model in a more realistic P&P grammar space, and discuss the desirable consequences in the reduction of computational cost.

The asymptotic properties of the $L_{R-P}$ model have been extensively studied in both mathematical psychology (Norman 1972) and machine learning (Narendra & Thathachar 1989, Barto & Sutton 1998). For simplicity but without loss of generality, suppose that there are two grammars in the population, $G_1$ and $G_2$, and that they are associated with penalty probabilities of $c_1$ and $c_2$ respectively. If the learning rate $\gamma$ is sufficiently small, i.e. the learner does not alter his 'confidence' in grammars too radically, one can show (see Narendra and Thathachar 1989: 162–5) that the asymptotic distributions of $p_1(t)$ and $p_2(t)$ will be essentially normal and can be approximated as follows:

(24)　**Theorem:**

$$\lim_{t \to \infty} p_1(t) = \frac{c_2}{c_1 + c_2}$$

$$\lim_{t \to \infty} p_2(t) = \frac{c_1}{c_1 + c_2}$$

(24) shows that in the general case, grammars more compatible with the input data are better represented in the population than those less compatible with the input data as the result of learning.

## 2.3.2　Stable multiple grammars

Recall from section 2.1.1 that realistic linguistic environments are usually heterogeneous, and the actual linguistic data cannot be attributed to a single idealized 'grammar'. This inherent variability poses a significant challenge for the robustness of the triggering model.

How does the variational model fare in realistic environments that are inherently variable? Observe that non-homogeneous linguistic expressions can be viewed as a probabilistic combination of expressions generated by multiple grammars. From a learning perspective, a non-homogeneous environment induces a population of grammars none of which is 100% compatible with the input data. The theorem in (24) shows that the weights of two (or more, in the general case) grammars reach a stable equilibrium when learning stops. Therefore, the variability of a speaker's linguistic competence can be viewed as a probabilistic combination of multiple grammars. We note in passing that this interpretation is similar to the concept of 'variable rules' (Labov 1969, Sankoff 1978), and may offer a way to integrate generative linguists' idealized grammars with the study of language variation and use in linguistic performance. In Chapter 5, we extend the acquisition model to language change. We show that a combination of grammars as the result of acquisition, while stable in a single (synchronic) generation of learners, may not be diachronically stable. We will derive certain conditions under which one grammar will inevitably replace another in a number of generations, much like the process of natural selection. This formalizes historical linguists' intuition of grammar competition as a mechanism for language change.

Consider the special case of an idealized environment in which all linguistic expressions are generated by an input grammar $G_1$. By definition, $G_1$ has a penalty probability of 0, while all other grammars in the population have positive penalty probabilities. It is easy to see from (24) that the $p_1$ converges to 1, with the competing grammars eliminated. Thus, the variational model meets the traditional learnability condition.

Empirically, one of the most important features of the variational model is its ability to make quantitative predictions about language development via the calculation of the expected change in the weights of the competing grammars. Again, consider two grammars, target $G_1$ and the competitor $G_2$, with $c_1 = 0$ and $c_2 > 0$. At any time, $p_1 + p_2 = 1$. With the presentation of each input sentence, the expected increase of $p_1$, $E[\Delta p_1]$, can be computed as follows:

(25) $E[\Delta p_1] = p_1\gamma(1-p_1) +$     with Pr. $p_1$, $G_1$ is chosen and $G_1 \to s$
$\phantom{E[\Delta p_1] =} p_2(1-c_2)(-\gamma)p_1 +$     with Pr. $p_2(1-c_2)$, $G_2$ is chosen and $G_2 \to s$
$\phantom{E[\Delta p_1] =} p_2 c_2 \gamma(1-p_1)$     with Pr. $p_2 c_2$, $G_2$ is chosen and $G_2 \not\to s$
$\phantom{E[\Delta p_1]} = c_2\gamma(1-p_1)$

## 34   A Variational Model

Although the actual rate of language development is hard to predict—it would rely on an accurate estimate of the learning parameter and the precise manner in which the learner updates grammar weights—the model does make *comparative* predictions on language development. That is, *ceteris paribus*, the rate at which a grammar is learned is determined by the penalty probability ($c_2$) of its competitor. By estimating penalty probabilities of grammars from CHILDES (25) allows us to make longitudinal predictions about language development that can be verified against actual findings. In Chapter 4, we do just that.

Before we go on, a disclaimer, or rather, a confession, is in order. We in fact are not committed to the $L_{R-P}$ model *per se*: exactly how children change grammar weights in response to their success or failure, as said earlier, is almost completely unknown. What we are committed to is the *mode* of learning: coexisting hypotheses in competition and gradual selection, as schematically illustrated in (18), and elaborated throughout this book with case studies in child language. The choice of the $L_{R-P}$ model is justified mainly because it allows the learner to converge to a stable equilibrium of grammar weights when the linguistic evidence is not homogeneous (24). This is needed to accommodate the fact of linguistic variation in adult speakers that is particularly clear in language change, as we shall see in Chapter 5. There are doubtlessly many other models with similar properties.

### 2.3.3   *Unambiguous evidence*

The theorem in (24) states that in the variational model, convergence to the target grammar is guaranteed if all competitor grammars have positive penalty probabilities. One way to ensure this is to assume the existence of unambiguous evidence (Fodor 1998): sentences that are compatible only with the target grammar, and not with any other grammar. While the general existence of unambiguous evidence has been questioned (Clark 1992, Clark &

Roberts 1993), the present model does not require unambiguous evidence to converge in any case.

To illustrate this, consider the following example. The target of learning is a Dutch V2 grammar, which competes in a population of (prototype) grammars, where X denotes an adverb, a prepositional phrase, and other adjuncts that can freely appear at the initial position of a sentence:

(26) a. Dutch: SVO, XVSO, OVS
 b. Hebrew: SVO, XVSO
 c. English: SVO, XSVO
 d. Irish: VSO, XVSO
 e. Hixkaryana: OVS, XOVS

The grammars in (26) are followed by some of the matrix sentences word orders they can generate/analyze.[11] Observe that none of the patterns in (26a) *alone* could distinguish Dutch from the other four human grammars, as each of them is compatible with certain V2 sentences. Specifically, based on the input evidence received by a Dutch child (Hein), we found that in declarative sentences, for which the V2 constraint is relevant, 64.7% are SVO patterns, followed by XVSO patterns at 34% and only 1.3% OVS patterns.[12] Most notably, Hebrew, and Semitic in general, grammar, which allows VSO and SVO alternations (Universal 6: Greenberg 1963; see also Fassi-Fehri 1993, Shlonsky 1997), is compatible with 98.7% of V2 sentences.

Despite the lack of unambiguous evidence for the V2 grammar, as long as SVO, OVS, and XVSO patterns appear at positive frequencies, all the competing grammars in (26) will be punished. The V2 grammar, however, is never punished. The theorem in (24) thus ensures the learner's convergence to the target V2 grammar. The competition of grammars is illustrated in Fig. 2.1, based on a computer simulation.

---

[11] For simplicity, we assume a degree-0 learner in the sense of Lightfoot (1991), for which we can find relevant corpus statistics in the literature.
[12] Thanks to Edith Kaan for her help in this corpus study.

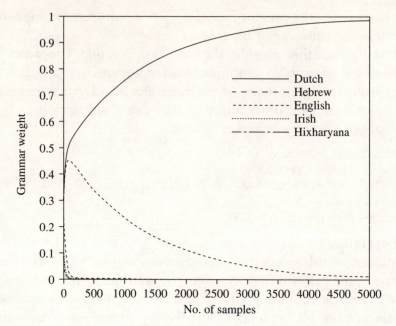

FIGURE 2.1. The convergence to the V2 grammar in the absence of unambiguous evidence

## 2.4 Learning grammars in a parametric space

The variational model developed in the preceding sections is entirely theory-neutral. It only requires a finite and non-arbitrary space of possible grammars, a conclusion accepted by many of today's linguists.[13] Some interesting questions arise when we situate the learning model in a realistic theory of grammar space, the P&P model.

### 2.4.1 Parameter interference

So far we have been treating competing grammars as individual entities; we have not taken into account the structure of the

---

[13] Different theories of UG will yield different generalizations: when situated into a theory-neutral learning model, they will—if they are not merely notational

grammar space. Although the convergence result in (24) for two grammars generalizes to any number of grammars, it is clear that when the number of grammars increases, the number of grammar weights that have to be stored also increases. According to some estimates (Clark 1992; cf. Kayne 2000, Baker 2001), 30–40 binary parameters are required to give a reasonable coverage of the UG space. And, if the grammars are stored as individual wholes, the learner would have to manipulate $2^{30}$–$2^{40}$ grammar weights: now *that* seems implausible.

It turns out that a parametric view of grammar variation, independently motivated by comparative theoretical linguistics, dramatically reduces the computational load of learning. Suppose that there are $n$ binary parameters, $\alpha_1, \alpha_2, \ldots, \alpha_n$, which can specify $2^n$ grammars. Each parameter $\alpha_i$ is associated with a weight $p_i$, the probability of the parameter $\alpha_i$ being 1. The weights constitute an $n$-dimensional vector of real numbers between $[0, 1]$: $\mathbf{P} = (p_1, p_2, \ldots, p_n)$.

Now the problem of selecting a grammar becomes the problem of selecting a vector of $n$ 0s and 1s, which can be done independently according to the parameter weights. For example, if the current value of $p_i$ is 0.7, then the learner has a 70% chance of selecting 1 and a 30% chance of selecting 0. As the value of $p_i$ changes, so will the probability of selecting 1 or 0. Now, given a current parameter weight vector $\mathbf{P} = (p_1, p_2, \ldots, p_n)$, the learner can non-deterministically generate a string of 0s and 1s, which is a grammar, $G$. Write this as $\mathbf{P} \Rightarrow G$, and the probability of $\mathbf{P} \Rightarrow G$ is the product of the parameter weights with respect to $G$'s parameter values. $\mathbf{P}$ gives rise to all $2^n$ grammars; as $\mathbf{P}$ changes, the probability of $\mathbf{P} \Rightarrow G$ also changes. When $\mathbf{P}$ reaches the target vector, then the probability of generating non-target grammars will be infinitely small.

(27) describes how $\mathbf{P}$ generates a grammar to analyze an incoming sentence:

---

variants—make different developmental predictions. The present model can then be used as an independent procedure to evaluate linguistic theories. See Ch. 6 for a brief discussion.

(27) For each incoming sentence $s$
    a. For parameter $i$, $i = 1, 2, \ldots, n$
       • with probability $p_i$, choose the value of $\alpha_i$ to be 1;
       • with probability $1 - p_i$, choose the value of $\alpha_i$ to be 0.
    b. Let $G$ be the grammar with the parameter values chosen in (27a).
    c. Analyze $s$ with $G$.
    d. Update the parameter values to $\mathbf{P}' = (p_1', p_2', \ldots, p_n')$ accordingly.

Now a problem of *parameter interference* immediately arises. Under the parametric representation of grammars, grammar selection is based on independent *parameters*. By contrast, fitness measure and thus the outcome of learning—reward or punishment—is defined on whole *grammars*. How does the learner infer, backwards, what to do with individual parameter weights, from their collective fitness as a composite grammar? In other words, what is the proper interpretation of *accordingly* in the parameter learning model (27)?

To be concrete, suppose we have two independent parameters: one determines whether the language has overt *Wh* movement (as in English but not Chinese), and the other determines whether the language has verb second (V2), generally taken to be the movement of inflected verbs to matrix Complementizer position, as in many Germanic languages. Suppose that the language to be acquired is German, which has [+Wh] and [+V2]. When the parameter combination [+Wh, −V2] is chosen, the learner is presented with a declarative sentence. Now although [+Wh] is the target value for the *Wh* parameter, the whole grammar [+Wh, −V2] is nevertheless incompatible with a V2 declarative sentence and will fail. But should the learner prevent the correct parameter value [+Wh] from being punished? If so, how? Similarly, the grammar [−Wh, +V2] will succeed at any declarative German sentence, and the wrong parameter value [−Wh], irrelevant to the input, may hitch a ride and get rewarded.

So the problem is this. The requirement of psychological plausibility forces us to cast grammar probability competition in terms of parameter probability competition. This in turns introduces the problem of parameter interference: updating independent parameter probability is made complicated by the success/failure of the composite grammar. In what follows, we will address this problem from several angles that, in combination, may yield a decent solution.

## 2.4.2 Independent parameters and signatures

To be sure, not all parameters are subject to the interference problem. Some parameters are independent of other parameters, and can be learned independently from a class of input examples that we will call *signatures*. Specifically, with respect to a parameter $\alpha$, its signature refers to $s_\alpha$, a class of sentences that are analyzable only if $\alpha$ is set to the target value. Furthermore, if the input sentence does not belong to $s_\alpha$, the value of $\alpha$ is not material to the analyzability of that sentence.

In the variational model, unlike the cue-based learning model to be reviewed a little later, the signature–parameter association need not be specified a priori, and neither does the learner actively search for signature in the input. Rather, signatures are interpreted as input whose cumulative effect leads to correct setting of parameters. Specifically, both values of a parameter are available to the child at the outset. The non-target value, however, is penalized upon the presentation of 'signatures', which, by definition, are only compatible with the target value. Hence, the non-target value has a positive penalty probability, and will be eliminated after a sufficient number of signatures have been encountered.

The existence of signatures for independent parameters is useful in two important ways. On the one hand, it radically reduces the problem of parameter interferences. For every parameter that is independent, the learning space is in effect cut by half; we will clarify this claim shortly, in section 2.4.4.[14] On the

---

[14] This also suggests that when proposing syntactic parameters, we should have the problem of acquisition in mind. When possible, parameters that can be independently learned better serve the goal of explanatory adequacy in reducing the cognitive load of child language acquisition.

other hand, parameters with signatures lead to longitudinal predictions that can be directly related to corpus statistics. For two such parameters, we can estimate the frequencies of their respective signature, and predict, on the basis of (25), that the parameter with more abundant signatures be learned sooner than the other. In Chapter 4, we will see the acquisition of several independent parameters that can be developmentally tracked this way.

So what *are* these independent parameters? Of the better-established parameters, a few are obviously independent. The *Wh* movement parameter is a straightforward example. *Wh* words move in English questions, but not in Chinese questions, and *Wh* questions will serve to unambiguously determine the target values of this parameter, regardless of the values of other parameters. For non-*Wh* sentences, the *Wh* parameter obviously has no effect.

Another independent parameter is the verb raising parameter that determines whether a finite verb raises to Tense: French sets this parameter to 1, and English, 0 (Emonds 1978, Pollock 1989). The 1 value for this parameter is associated with signature such as (28), where finite verbs precede negation/adverb:[15]

(28) a. Jean ne mange pas de fromage.
Jean *ne* eats    no of cheese.
'John does not eat cheese.'
b. Jean mange souvent du fromage.
Jean eats    often    of cheese.
'John often eats cheese.'

Yet another independent parameter is the obligatory subject parameter, for which the positive value (e.g. English) is associated with the use of pure expletives such as *there* in sentences like *There is a train in the house*.

---

[15] Although it is possible that the verb does not stop at Tense but raises further to higher nodes (as in verb-second environments), the principle of the Head Movement Constraint (Travis 1984), or more generally economy conditions (Chomsky 1995b), would prohibit such raising to skip the intermediate Tense node. Therefore, finite verbs followed by negation or adverbs in a language indicate that the verb must raise at least to Tense.

What about the parameters are not independent, whose values can not be directly determined by any particular type of input data? In section 2.4.3 we review two models that untangle parameter interference by endowing the learner with additional resources. We then propose, in section 2.4.4, a far simpler model and study its formal sufficiency. Our discussion is somewhat technical; the disinterested reader can go straight to section 2.5. A fuller treatment of the mathematical and computational issues can be found in Yang (in press).

## 2.4.3 *Interference avoidance models*

One approach is to give the learner the ability to tease out the relevance of parameters with respect of an input sentence. Fodor's (1998) Structural Trigger Learner (STL) takes this approach. The STL has access to a special parser that can detect whether an input sentence is parametrically ambiguous. If so, the present parameter values are left unchanged; parameters are set only when the input is completely unambiguous. The STL thus aims to avoid the local maxima problem, caused by parametric inference, in Gibson & Wexler's triggering model.[16]

The other approach was proposed by Dresher & Kaye (1990) and Dresher (1999); see Lightfoot (1999) for an extension to the acquisition of syntax. They note that the parameters in metrical stress can be associated with a corresponding set of *cues*, input data that can unambiguously determine the values of the parameters in a language. Dresher & Kaye (1990) propose that for each parameter, the learner is innately endowed with the knowledge of the cue associated with that parameter. In addition, each parameter has a *default* value, which is innately specified as well. Upon the presentation of a cue, the learner sets the value for the corresponding parameter. Crucially, cues are *ordered*. That is, the cue

---

[16] Tesar & Smolensky Constraint Demotion model (2000) is similar. For them, a pair of violable constraints is (re)ordered only when their relative ranking can be unambiguously determined from an input datum; the detection of ambiguity involves examining other candidate rankings.

for a parameter may not be usable if another parameter has not been set. This leads to a particular sequence of parameter setting, which must be innately specified. Suppose the parameter sequence is $\alpha_1, \alpha_2, \ldots \alpha_n$, associated with cues $s_1, s_2, \ldots, s_n$, respectively. (29) schematically shows the mechanisms of the cue-based learner:

(29) a. Initialize $\alpha_1, \alpha_2, \ldots, \alpha_n$ with their respective default values.
 b. For $i = 1, 2, \ldots, n$
  - Set $\alpha_i$ upon seeing $s_i$.
  - Leave the set parameters $\alpha_1, \ldots, \alpha_{n-1}$ alone.
  - Reset $\alpha_{i+1}, \ldots, \alpha_n$ to respective default values.

In the present context, we do not discuss the formal sufficiency of the STL and the cue-based models.[17] The STL model seems to introduce computational cost that is too high to be realistic: the learner faces a very large degree of structural ambiguity that must be disentangled (Sakas & Fodor 2001). The cue-based model would only work if *all* parameters are associated with cues and default values, and the order in which parameters are set must be identified as well. While this has been deductively worked out for about a dozen parameters in metrical stress (Dresher 1999), whether the same is true for a non-trivial space of syntactic parameters remains to be seen.

Both models run into problems with the developmental compatibility condition, detrimental to all transformational learning models: they cannot capture the variation in and the gradualness of language development. The STL model may maintain that before a parameter is conclusively set, both parameter values are available, to which variation in child language are be attributed. However, when a parameter *is* set, it is set in an all-or-none fashion, which then incorrectly predicts abrupt changes in child language.

The cue-based model is completely deterministic. At any time,

---

[17] Both have problems: see Bertolo et al. (1997) for a formal discussion; see also Church (1992) for general comments on the cue-based model, and Gillis et al. (1995) for a computer simulation.

a parameter is associated with a unique parameter value—correct or incorrect, but not both—and hence no variation in child language can be accounted for. In addition, the unset parameters are reset to default values every time a parameter is set. This predicts radical and abrupt reorganization of child language: incorrectly, as reviewed earlier. Finally, the cue-based model entails that learners of all languages will follow an identical learning path, the order in which parameters are set: we have not been able to evaluate this claim.

## 2.4.4 Naive parameter learning

In what follows, we will pursue an approach that sticks to the strategy of assuming a 'dumb' learner.[18] Consider the algorithm in (30), a *Naive Parameter Learner* (NPL):

(30) Naive Parameter Learning (NPL)
    a. Reward *all* the parameter values if the composite grammar succeeds.
    b. Punish *all* the parameter values if the composite grammar fails.

The NPL model may reward wrong parameter values as hitchhikers, and punish correct parameter values as accomplices. The hope is that, in the long run, the correct parameter values will prevail.

To see how (30) works, consider again the learning of the two parameters [Wh] and [V2] in a German environment. The combinations of the two parameters give four grammars, of which we can explicitly measure the fitness values (penalty probabilities). Based on the CHILDES corpus, we estimate that about 30% of all sentences children hear are Wh questions,[19] which are only compatible with the [+Wh] value. Of the remaining declarative sentences, about 49% are SVO sentences that are consistent with the [−V2] value. The other 21% are VS sentences with a topic

---

[18] For useful discussions I would like to thank Sam Gutmann, Julie Legate, and in particular Morgan Sonderegger for presenting our joint work here.
[19] This figure is based on English data: we are taking the liberty to extrapolate it to our (hypothetical) German simulation.

in [Spec,CP], which are only compatible with the [+V2] value. We then have the penalty probabilities shown in Table 2.1.

Fig. 2.2 shows the changes of the two parameter values over time. We see that the two parameters, which fluctuated in earlier stages of learning—the target values were punished and the non-target values were rewarded—converged correctly to [1, 1] in the end.

It is not difficult to prove that for parameters with signatures, the NPL will converge on the target value, using the Martingale methods in Yang & Gutmann (1999); see Yang (in press) for

TABLE 2.1. The penalty probabilities of four grammars composed of two parameters

|        | [+Wh] | [−Wh] |
|--------|-------|-------|
| [+V2]  | 0     | 0.3   |
| [−V2]  | 0.21  | 0.51  |

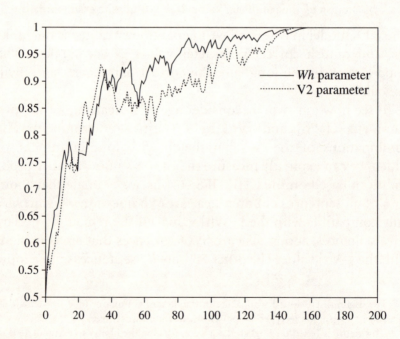

FIGURE 2.2. The independent learning of two parameters, Wh and V2

details. We now turn to the more difficult issue of learning parameters that are subject to the interference problem.

Fitness distribution

In what follows, we will suggest that (some variant) of the NPL may be a plausible model of learning that distangles the interference effects from parameter interaction.

First, our conclusion is based on results from computer simulation. This is not the preferred move, for the obvious reason that one cannot simulate all possibilities that may arise in parameter learning. Analytical results—proofs—are much better, but so far they have been elusive.

Second, as far as feasible, we will study the behavior of the model in an *actual* learning environment. As the example of the Wh and V2 learning (Fig. 2.2) shows, the relative fitness values of the four composite grammars will determine the outcome of parameter learning. In that example, if the three competitors have high penalty probabilities, intuition tells us that the two parameters rise to target values quickly.[20] So the actual behavior of the model can be understood only if we have a good handle on the fitness distribution of actual grammars.

This is a departure from the traditional linguistic learnability study, and we believe it is a necessary one. Learnability models, in general, do not consider convergence in relation to the actual (statistical) distribution of the learning data.[21] Rather, learning is studied 'in the limit' (Gold 1967), with the assumption that learning can take an arbitrary amount of data as long as it converges on the correct grammar in the end: hence, no sample complexity considerations. However, it is clear that learning data is not infinite. In Chapter 4 we show that it is possible to establish bounds on the amount of linguistic data needed for actual acquisition: if

---

[20] Although intuition fades rapidly as more and more parameters combine and interact.

[21] A notable exception is Berwick & Niyogi's (1996) elegant Markov model of triggering, where the expected amount of evidence required for convergence can be precisely worked out.

the learning data required by a model greatly exceed such bounds, then such a model will fail the formal sufficiency condition.

Sample complexity, even if it *is* formally studied, means very little unless placed in an actual context. For example, suppose one has found models that require exactly $n$ or $n^2$ specific kinds of input sentences to set $n$ parameters. The sample complexity of this model is very small: a (low) polynomial function of the problem size. But to claim this is an efficient model, one must show that these $n^2$ sentences are in fact *attested* with robust frequencies in the actual input: a model whose theoretical convergence relies on twenty levels of embedded clauses with parasitic gaps is hopeless in reality.

In a similar vein, a model that fails under some hypothetical conditions may not be doomed either: it is possible that such cases never arise in actual learning environments. For example, computer simulation shows that the NPL model does not converge onto the target parameter values in a reasonable amount of time if all of the $2^n - 1$ composite grammars have the penalty probability of 0.1: that is, all non-target grammars are equally good, compatible with 90% of input data. But this curious (and disastrous) scenario does not occur in reality.

It is very difficult to know what actual penalty probability distributions are like. To do so, one would have to consider all, at least a large portion, of the $2^n$ grammars. For each grammar, which is a parameter value vector, one needs to find a corresponding existing language, take a large sample of sentences from it, and then analyze the sample with all the other $2^n - 1$ competitors. It is obvious that each of these steps poses enormous practical problems for large numbers of $n$. Our experience working with corpora (Chapter 4) suggests that there are relatively few competing grammars with low penalty probabilities, i.e. very close to the target grammar, whereas the vast majority of them are bad. The example in (26), the V2 grammar in competition with four other grammars, is a case in point. This assumption seems compatible with the fact that most (but not all) parameters are acquired fairly early, which would not be possible if the relative compatibilities among grammars were very high.

Furthermore, we believe that it is reasonable to assume that the badness of a grammar is in general correlated with how 'far away' it is from the target grammar, where distance can be measured by how many parameter values they differ: the Hamming distance. In particular, we assume that as grammars get further and further away, their fitness values deteriorate rapidly. It is true that the change of *some* parameter may induce radical changes on the overall grammar obtained, e.g. [±Wh], scrambling (though some of these parameters may be independent, and thus free of parameter interference). Hence, what we assume is only a statistical tendency: it is possible that a grammar closer to the target (in terms of the Hamming distance) is worse than one that is further away, but it is unlikely.

Specifically, we assume that the penalty probabilities of the competing grammars follow a standard Gaussian distribution:

(31) $\quad c(x) = 1 - e^{-\frac{x^2}{2\sigma^2}}$, where $\sigma = 1/3$

To choose penalty probabilities, we first divide the interval (0, 1) into $n$ equal segments, where $n$ is the number of parameters. A grammar $G_h$ with Hamming distance $h$ is expected to fall in the $h$th interval. However, to simulate the effect that grammars further from the target are generally (but not always) worse than the closer ones, we assume that $G_h$ falls in the $h$th region with probability $s$, in the $h \pm$ 1st regions with probability $s^2$, in the $h \pm$ 2nd regions with probability $s^3$, etc. This is our assumption of *exponential decay* of grammar fitness with respect to its Hamming distance. Thus, a grammar farther away can be still be compatible with many sentences from the target grammar, but the likelihood of it being so vanishes very quickly. Similarly, a grammar that differs from the target by few paprameters can also be fairly bad. But overall, further away grammars are on average worse than those that are closer to the target.

To verify our assumptions of penalty probability distributions, we consider a very small case, for $n = 3$ with three parameters, in Gibson & Wexler (1994): Spec-Head, Comp-Head, and V2. And even here we will make simplified assumptions; see Appendix A for details. First, we only consider the matrix clauses, as in Gibson & Wexler (1994). Second, some essential distributional statistics are based on English and Germanic languages, and then extrapolated (not unreasonably, we believe) to other grammars. Averaging over the pairwise penalty probabilities of eight grammars, we have:

(32)   a. The average penalty probability for grammars one parameter away is 0.571312.
       b. The average penalty probability for grammars two parameters away is 0.687908.
       c. The average penalty probability for grammars three parameters away is 0.727075.

This is clearly consistent with our assumption about fitness distribution. Penalty probability in general correlates with the Hamming distance from the target. The pairwise penalty probabilities (Table 2.3 in Appendix A) are also consistent with our assumption of distance-related exponential decay.

### 2.4.5 Learning rates and random walks

If one runs the NPL on the distribution of penalty probabilities as in (31), a number of problems arise, all having to do with the choice of the learning parameter, $\gamma$, which controls the rapidity with which the learner adjusts the parameters. First, if $\gamma$ is too small—the learner modifies parameter weights very slightly upon success/failure—the learner takes an incredibly long time to converge. And second, if $\gamma$ is too big, the learner will modify the parameter weights very abruptly, resulting in a 'jumpy' learning curve, not so unlike the original triggering model rejected on the ground of developmental incompatibility (section 2.1.2).

It is not hard to understand why this may be the case. Consider the current parameter weight vector $\mathbf{P} = (p_1, p_2, \ldots, p_n)$, and the target values are $\mathbf{T}$, which is an $n$-ary vector of 0s and 1s. When $\mathbf{P}$ is far from $\mathbf{T}$, e.g. $\mathbf{P} = (0.5, 0.5, \ldots, 0.5)$, the learner has no idea what $\mathbf{T}$ may be. As $\mathbf{P}$ gets closer to $\mathbf{T}$, the learner will be able to analyze incoming sentences more often. Thus, the learner may have increasingly higher confidence in **P**, which now works better and better. It then seems reasonable to assume that the learner ought to be more conservative when **P** is far from the target, but more assured when **P** gets close.

There are a number of ways of implementing this intuition. One may assume that the gradual increase in $\gamma$ is a matter of biological maturation. There are also many algorithms in computer science and machine learning that formally—and computationally expensively—modify the learning rate with respect to the confidence interval. But these approaches will alter the mathematical properties of the $L_{R-P}$ model (22), which requires a fixed learning rate. Furthermore, they deviate from the guidelines of psychological plausibility and explanatory continuity that acquisition models are advised to follow (Chapter 1).

An alternative is suggested by Morgan Sonderegger (personal communication). It is based on two observations. First, note that having a high $\gamma$ is equivalent to having a fixed $\gamma$ and *using it* often. Second, the overall goodness of **P** can be related to how often **P** successfully analyzes incoming sentences. This leads to a very simple measure of how close **P** is to the target, by introducing a small batch counter $b$, which is initialized to 0, and a batch bound $B$, a small positive integer (usually between 2 and 5, in practice). Formally,

(33) The Naive Parameter Learner with Batch (NPL+B)
 a. For an input sentence $s$, select a grammar $G$ based on **P** following the procedure in (27)
 b. • If $G \to s$, then $b = b + 1$.
    • If $G \not\to s$, then $b = b - 1$.
 c. • If $b = B$, reward $G$ and reset $b = 0$.
    • If $b = -B$, punish $G$ and reset $b = 0$.
 d. Go to (33a).

Note that the use of 'batch' in NPL+B (33) is very different from the standard one. Usually, 'batch' refers to a memory that stores a number of data points before processing them. In NPL+B, $b$ is simply a counter that tracks the success or failure of sentence analysis, without recording what sentences have been presented or what grammars selected. The cost of additional memory load is trivial.

Yet the effect of this batch is precisely what we wanted: it slows down the learning rate when **P** is bad, and speeds it up when **P** gets better. To see this, consider that **P** is very close to **T**. Now almost every sentence is compatible with the grammars given by **P**, because most of the non-target grammars now have a very low probability of being selected. Then, almost every $B$ sentences will push the batch counter $b$ to its bound ($B$). Weights will be updated very frequently, driving **P** to **T** ever more rapidly. By contrast, if **P** is quite far from **T**, then it generally takes a longer time for $b$ to reach its bound—reward and punishment are then less frequent, and thus slow down learning.

This batch process can be understood precisely by considering the problem of the Gambler's Ruin. A gambler has $n$ dollars to start the game. Every bet he makes, there is a probability $p$ of making a dollar, and a probability $q = 1 - p$ of losing a dollar. The gambler *wins* if he ends up with $2n$ dollars, and is ruined if he is down to 0. Since every gamble is independent of all others, the gambler's fortune takes a random walk. It is not difficult to show—the interested reader may consult any textbook on stochastic processes—that the probability of the gambler winning (i.e. getting $2n$ dollars), $w$, is:

$$(34) \quad w = \frac{(q/p)^n - 1}{(q/p)^{2n} - 1}$$

Our batch counter $b$ does exactly the same thing. It gains 1 when **P** yields a succesful grammar, and loses 1 when **P** yields a failing grammar. $b$ wins if it reaches $B$, and loses if it reaches $-B$. Let $p$ be the probability of **P** yielding a successful grammar.[22]

---

[22] Precisely, $p = \Sigma_i \Pr(\mathbf{P} \Rightarrow G_i)(1 - c_i)$, where $G_i$ is a grammar that can be generated by **P** (there are $2^n$ such grammars), where $n$ is the number of parameters, $\Pr(\mathbf{P} \Rightarrow G_i)$ is the probability that **P** generates the grammar $G_i$ (see (27)), and $c_i$ is the penalty probability of $G_i$.

Then $w_B$, the probability of $b$ reaching the batch bound $B$ is

(35) $\quad w(B, p) = \dfrac{(q/p)^B - 1}{(q/p)^{2B} - 1}$

Clearly, as $p$ gets bigger, $w_B$ gets larger, and as $B$ increases, $w_B$ gets larger still. Fig. 2.3 shows $w(B, p)$ as a function of $B$ and $p$. $B = 1$ means that there is no batch: the learning parameter would be uniform throughout learning.

The assumptions of the normal distribution of grammar fitness, the exponential decay of fitness with respect to the Hamming distance, and the use of a small batch counter together give rise to a satisfactory learner, the NPL+B model.[23] A typical result from a simulation of learning a ten-parameter grammar is given in Fig. 2.4.

The learning curve is generally smooth, with no abrupt changes. And the learner converges in a reasonable amount of time. About 600,000 sentences were needed for converging on ten interacting parameters.

It must be conceded that the formal sufficiency condition of the NPL model is only tentatively established. Future research lies in two directions. First, and obviously, much more work is needed to establish whether the assumptions of Gaussian distribution and exponential decay are accurate. Second, one may (manually) determine how many parameters are in fact independent, and thus do not lead to parameter interference.[24]

The most important consequence of the NLP model, if vindicated, lies in the dramatic reduction of computational cost: the memory load reduced from storing $2^n$ grammar weights to $n$ parameter weights. This makes the variational model psychologically plausible, and in turn gives a computational argument for the conception of UG as a parametric space.

---

[23] A copy of the NPL+B learner can be obtained from the author.
[24] If abundant, then it is good news for the STL model (Fodor 1998, Sakas & Fodor 2001). Presumably, the learner can focus on parameters that are not independent: a smaller space means smaller computational cost for the STL parser.

## 52  A Variational Model

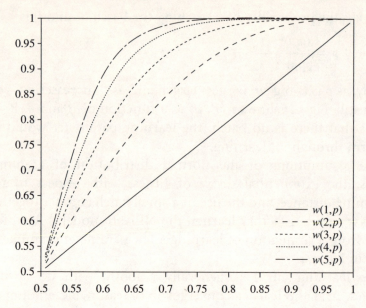

FIGURE 2.3. The probability function $w(B, p) = \dfrac{(q/p)^B - 1}{(q/p)^{2B} - 1}$

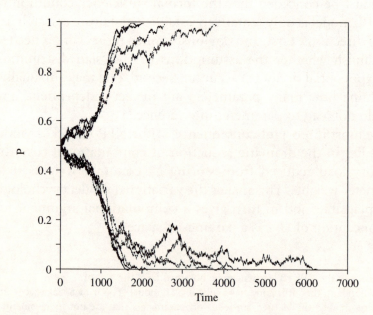

FIGURE 2.4.  NPL+B learning of the grammar (1 0 0 0 0 1 0 1 1 0). $B = 5$, $\gamma = 0.002$, $s = 5/6$

Learning in a parametric space gives rise to 'hybrid' grammars. Since the successful acquisition of a grammar is accomplished only when all parameters are set correctly, children may go through an extended period of time in which some parameters are already in place while others are still fluctuating. For example, an English child may have learned that his language moves *Wh* words overtly, but has not conclusively learned that it also obligatorily uses overt subjects. Now what the child possesses are partial fragments of grammars that may not correspond to any attested adult language—something that is, say, English-like in one respect but Chinese-like in another. And it is precisely these hybrid languages that confirms the reality of grammar coexistence and competition. A number of such cases in child languages will be documented in Chapter 4.

## 2.5  Related approaches

The idea of language acquisition as grammar competition has occasionally surfaced in the literature, although it has never been pursued systematically or directly related to quantitative data in language development.

To the best of our knowledge, Jakobson (1941) was the first to interpret 'errors' in child phonology as possible phonological forms in non-target adult languages. This position was echoed in Stampe (1979), and seems to be accepted by at least some researchers in phonological acquisition (Macken 1995). Recent studies on infants' gradual loss of universal ability for phonetic discrimination (Kuhl et al. 1992; cf. de Boysson-Bardies 1999) seem to suggest that the variational model, in which the hypothesis space goes from 'more' to 'less' through competition, may hint at a general process that also governs the development of phonetic perception.

Since the advent of the P&P framework, some linguists have claimed that syntactic acquisition selects a grammar out of all possible human grammars (Piattelli-Palmarini 1989, Lightfoot 1991), but nothing has been formalized. That children may have simultaneous access to multiple hypotheses has been suggested by Berwick & Weinberg (1984) and Pinker (1984), among others. The possibility of associating grammars with weights has been raised by Valian (1990), Weinberg (1990), and Bloom (1993), either for learnability considerations or to explain the gradual developmental patterns in child language. These authors, however, opted for different solutions to the problems under study.

Recently, Roeper (2000; cf. Yang 2000) has independently proposed that child language be explained as a combination of multiple grammars simultaneously available to the learner. Roeper further suggests that in the selection of competing grammars, the learner follows some principles of economy akin to those in the Minimalist Program (Chomsky 1995b): grammars with less complex structural representations are preferred.[25] Roeper gives evidence for the view of multiple grammars. For instance, English children who alternate between *I go*, using a nominative case subject, and *me go*, using a default (accusative) case, can be viewed as using two grammars with different case/agreement systems, both of which are attested in human languages.

The genetic algorithm (GA) model of Clark (1992) is most similar to the present model. The GA model represents grammars as parameter vectors, which undergo reproduction via 'crossover', i.e. parts of two parental parameter vectors are swapped and combined.[26] A mutation process is also assumed which, with some probability, randomly flips bits in the grammar vector. Candidate grammars are evaluated against input data; hence, measure of fitness is defined, which is subsequently translated into differential reproduction.

---

[25] The present model is presented in the most general way: all grammars are there to begin with, and input-grammar compatibility is the only criterion for rewarding/punishing grammars. It can incorporate other possibilities, including the economy condition suggested by Roeper. For instance, one can build in some appropriate prior bias in grammar evaluation—analyzability of $G \rightarrow s$ in (22)—that goes against complex grammars. However, these additional biases must be argued for empirically.

[26] This operation seems to require some empirical justification.

Both the GA model and the variational model are explicitly built on the idea of language acquisition as grammar competition; and in both models, grammars are selected for or against on the basis of their compatibility with input data. There are, however, a few important differences. One major difference lies in the evaluation of grammar fitness. In the present model, the fitness of a grammar is defined as its penalty probability, an extensional notion that is only used to described the dynamics of learning. It is not accessed by the learner, but can be measured from text corpora by the linguist. In the GA model, the learner first computes the degree of parsability for all grammars over a large sample of sentences. The parsability measures are then explicitly used to determine the differential reproduction that leads to the next generation of grammars. The computational cost associated with fitness evaluation is too large to be plausible. The variational model developed here sidesteps these problems by making use of probabilities/weights to capture the cumulative effects of discriminating linguistic evidence.

In the following chapters, we will pursue the condition of developmental compatibility and present a diverse array of evidence to support the variational model.

## Appendix A: Fitness distribution in a three-parameter space

Gibson & Wexler (1994: table 3) considered the variations of degree-0 sentences within three parameters: Spec-Head, Comp-Head, and V2. The strings are composed of Subject, Verb, Object, Double Objects, Auxiliary, and Adverb (which broadly refers to adjuncts or topics that quite freely appear in the initial position of a sentence). For simplicity, we do not consider double objects. The grammars and the patterns they can generate are given in Table 2.2.

A principled way to estimate the probability of a string $w_1^n = w_1, w_2 \ldots w_n$ is to compute its joint probability by the use of the Chain Rule:

TABLE 2.2. A space of three parameters, or eight grammars, and the string patterns they allow

| Language | Spec-Head | Comp-Head | V2 | degree-0 sentences |
| --- | --- | --- | --- | --- |
| VOS–V2 | 1 | 1 | 0 | VS VOS AVS AVOS<br>XVS XVOS XAVOS |
| VOS+V2 | 1 | 1 | 1 | SV SVO OVS SV SAVO OAVS<br>XVS XVOS XAVS XAVOS |
| SVO–V2 | 0 | 1 | 0 | SV SVO SAV SAVO<br>XSV XSVO XSAV XSAVO |
| SVO+V2 | 0 | 1 | 1 | SV SVO OVS SAV SAVO OASV<br>XVS XVSO XASV XASVO |
| OVS–V2 | 1 | 0 | 0 | VS OVS VAS OVAS<br>XVS XOVS XVAS XOVAS |
| OVS+V2 | 1 | 0 | 1 | SV OVS SVO SAV SAOV OAVS<br>XVS XVOS XAVS XAOVS |
| SOV–V2 | 0 | 0 | 0 | SV SOV SVA SOVA<br>XSOV XSVA XSOVA |
| SOV+V2 | 0 | 0 | 1 | SV SVO OVS SAV SAOV OASV<br>XVS XVSO XASV XASOV |

$$p(w_1^n) = p(w_1)p(w_2|w_1)p(w_3|w_1^2) \ldots p(w_n|w_1^{n-1}) = \prod_{k=1}^{n}(w_k|w_1^{k-1})$$

where the conditional probabilities can be estimated individually. For example, if $w_1 = S$, $w_2 = V$, and $w_3 = O$, then $p(SVO) = p(S)p(V|S)p(O|SV)$. It is easy to estimate $p(S)$: $p(S) = 1$ for obligatory subject languages, and $p(S) < 1$ for subject drop languages. Presumably $p(V|S) = 1$: every sentence has a verb (including auxiliary verbs). And $p(O|SV)$ is simply the frequency of transitive verb uses. When the $n$ gets large, the conditional probabilities get complicated, as substrings of $w_1 \ldots w_n$ are dependent. However, even with a very modest $n$, say, 10, one can get a fairly comprehensive coverage of sentential patterns (Kohl 1999). And again there is independence to be exploited; for example, verb-to-tense raising parameter is conditioned only upon the presence of a negation or adverb, and nothing else.

The crucial assumption we make is that there are similarities in the distributions of $w_i$s across languages, no matter how these languages put them together. It does not seem unreasonable to assume, say, that the frequencies of transitive verbs are more or less uniform across languages, because transitive verbs are used in certain life contexts, which perhaps do not vary greatly across languages. Practically, such assumptions are necessary if there is any hope of estimating the distribution of sentences in many grammars, without reliable parsers or comprehensive corpora. Furthermore, some grammars, i.e. parameter settings, may not be attested in the world.

Given these assumptions, let us see how we may estimate the string distributions for eight grammars in Table 2.2, extrapolating from the grammars for which we do have some statistical results. For the English grammar (SVO–V2), we estimate, using sources like the CHILDES corpus, that about 10% of declarative sentences have an sentence-initial XP; thus 90% of the probability mass will be distributed among SV, SVO, SAV, SAVO. Roughly 50% of all sentences contain an auxiliary, and 50% of verbs are transitives. Assuming that the selection of Auxiliary and Verb is independent, and that the selection of the XP adjunct is independent of the rest of the sentence. We then obtain:

(36)  a.   P(SV) = P(SVO) = P(SAV) = P(SAVO) = 9/40
      b.   P(XSV) = P(XSVO) = P(SAV) = P(XSAVO) = 1/40

(36) will be carried over to the other three non-V2 grammars, and assigned to their respective canonical word orders.

For the four V2 grammars, we assume that (36) will carry over to the canonical patterns due to the Spec-Head and Comp-Head parameters. In addition, we must consider the effect of V2: raising S, O, or X to the sentence-initial position. It is known from (Lightfoot 1997: 265) as well as from our own analysis of a Dutch adult-to-child corpus, that in V2 languages, S occupies the initial position 70% of time, X, 28%, and O, 2%. These probability masses (0.7, 0.28, and 0.02) will be distributed among the canonical patterns.

Putting these together, we may compute the penalty probability $c_{ij}$ of grammar $G_i$ relative to grammar $G_j$:

$$c_{ij} = \sum_{G_j \to s} P(s|G_i \not\to s)$$

The pairwise $c_{ij}$s are given in Table 2.3.

TABLE 2.3. Relative penalty probabilities of the eight grammars

| $C_{ij}$ | $G_{110}$ | $G_{111}$ | $G_{100}$ | $G_{101}$ | $G_{010}$ | $G_{011}$ | $G_{000}$ | $G_{001}$ |
|---|---|---|---|---|---|---|---|---|
| $G_{110}$ | – | 0.790 | 1.000 | 0.930 | 0.750 | 0.860 | 0.800 | 0.930 |
| $G_{111}$ | 0.900 | – | 0.100 | 0.220 | 0.750 | 0.245 | 0.625 | 0.395 |
| $G_{100}$ | 0.999 | 0.300 | – | 0.300 | 1.000 | 0.475 | 0.600 | 0.475 |
| $G_{101}$ | 0.966 | 0.220 | 0.100 | – | 0.750 | 0.395 | 0.625 | 0.245 |
| $G_{010}$ | 0.742 | 0.920 | 1.000 | 0.920 | – | 0.920 | 0.800 | 0.920 |
| $G_{011}$ | 0.933 | 0.245 | 0.325 | 0.395 | 0.750 | – | 0.625 | 0.220 |
| $G_{000}$ | 0.999 | 0.825 | 0.750 | 0.825 | 1.000 | 0.825 | – | 0.825 |
| $G_{001}$ | 0.967 | 0.395 | 0.325 | 0.245 | 0.750 | 0.200 | 0.625 | – |

Currently, we are extending these methods to grammars in a larger parametric space, based on the work of Kohl (1999).

# 3

# Rules over Words

> Fuck these irregular verbs.
> Quang Phuc Dong, *English Sentences without Overt Grammatical Subject* (1971), p. 4

The acquisition of English past tense has generated much interest and controversy in cognitive science, often pitched as a clash between generative linguistics and connectionism (Rumelhart & McClelland 1986), or even between rationalism and empiricism (Pinker 1999). This is irregular: the problem of past tense, particularly in English, notorious for its impoverished phonology, is a marginal problem in linguistics, and placing it at the center of attention does no justice to the intricacy of the study of language; see e.g. Halle (2000), Yang (2000), and Embick & Marantz (in press).

Yet this is not to say the problem of English past tense is trivial or uninteresting. As we shall see, despite the enthusiasm and efforts on both sides of the debate, there remain many important patterns in the published sources still unknown and unexplained. We show that the variational learning model, instantiated here as competition among phonological rules (rather than grammars/parameters, as in the case of syntactic acquisition), provides a new understanding of how phonology is organized and learned.

## 3.1 Background

Our problem primarily concerns three systematic patterns in children's acquisition of past tense. First, it has been known since

Berko's (1958) classic work that in general, children (and adults) inflect novel verbs with the *-d* suffix, as in *rick-ricked*. Second, young children sometimes *overregularize*: for example, they produce *take-taked* instead of *take-took*, where the suffix *-d* for regular verbs is used for an irregular verb. On average, overregularization occurs in about 10% of all instances of irregular verbs, according to the most extensive study of past tense acquisition (Marcus et al. 1992). Third, errors such as *bring-brang* and *wipe-wope*, mis-irregularization errors where children misapply and overapply irregular past tense forms, are exceeding rare, accounting for about 0.2% of all instances of irregular verb uses (Xu & Pinker 1995).

One leading approach to the problem of past tense, following the influential work of Rumelhart and McClelland (1986), claims that the systematic patterns noted above emerge from the statistical properties of the input data presented to connectionist networks. A number of problems with the connectionist approach have been identified (e.g. Fodor & Pylyshyn 1988, Lachter & Bever 1988, Pinker & Prince 1988, Marcus et al. 1992). To give just one example (from Prasada & Pinker 1993), connectionist models have difficulty with the *Wug*-test, the hallmark of past tense knowledge. When novel verbs such as *slace* and *smeeb* are presented to a trained connectionist model, *fraced* and *imin* are produced as their respective past tense forms, a behavior hopelessly incompatible with human performance.

In this chapter, we will critically assess another leading approach to the problem of past tense, the Words and Rule (WR) model developed by Pinker and his associates (Pinker 1995, 1999). The WR model claims that the computational system for past tense consists of two components. In the 'rule' component, following the tradition of generative linguistics, regular verbs are inflected by making use of a default phonological rule, which adds *-d* to the root (stem). This explains the productivity of *-d* suffixation to novel verbs. Equally important to the WR model is the Blocking Principle, a traditional idea dating back to Pāṇini. In past tense formation, the Blocking Principle has the effect of forcing the use of a more specific form over a more general form: for example, *sang* is a more specific realization of the past tense of *sing* than *singed*, and is therefore used. Irregular verbs are learned in the 'word' component, which works like a connectionist network, by direct association/memorization of the pairing between a stem and its past tense. The strength of association is conditioned upon the frequencies of irregular verbs that children hear; thus, memorization of irregular verbs takes time and experience to be perfected. When the child's memory for an irregular form fails, the default *-d* form is used. This accounts for the second salient pattern of past tense acquisition: overregularization errors in child language.

Here we will put forward an alternative approach, the Rules and Competition (RC) model. The RC model treats both irregular and regular verbs within a single component of the cognitive system: generative phonology. Like the WR model, we assume the presence of a default rule, which attaches the *-d* suffix to the stem and in principle applies to all verbs. In contrast to the WR model, we claim that irregular past tense is also formed by phonological rules. That is, errors such as overregularization are not memory lapses, but result from failures to apply appropriate *irregular* phonological rules over the default rule.

The RC model derives from the variational approach to language acquisition, which holds that systematic errors in child language are reflections of coexisting hypotheses in competition. These hypotheses are associated with weights, and it is the weights, or the distribution of the grammars, that change during learning from data. For the problem of past tense, the hypothesis space for each irregular verb $x$ includes an irregular rule $R$, defined over a verb class $S$ of verbs of which $x$ is a member. For example, the rule [*-t* suffixation & Vowel Shortening] applies to irregular verbs such as *lose*, *deal*, and *dream*. The acquisition of $x$ involves a process of competition between $R$ and the default *-d* rule, the latter of which in principle could apply to all verbs, regular and irregular. The child learns from experience that for irregular verbs, irregular rules must apply, and thus the default *-d* rule must not. Before learning is complete, the default rule will be probabilistically accessed, leading to overregularization errors.

Section 3.2 presents the RC model in detail, including a description of the past tense formation rules in the computational system and a learning algorithm that specifies how rules compete. We will also give a learning-theoretic interpretation and revision of the Blocking Principle that underlies the WR model as well as much of generative phonology. Section 3.3 compares the WR and RC models, based on the child acquisition data reported in Marcus et al. (1992). Specifically, we show that children's performance on an irregular verb strongly correlates with the weight of its corresponding phonological rule, which explains a number of class-based patterns in the acquisition of irregular verbs. These patterns receive no explanation under the WR model, to the extent that the WR model is explicitly formulated. Section 3.4 examines, and rejects, the proposal of pairing stem and past tense with analogy or phonological similarity in the WR model, which one might consider a partial remedy for the problems revealed in section 3.3. Section 3.5 gives a critical review of ten arguments in support of the WR model (Pinker 1995). We show that each of them is either empirically flawed or can be accommodated equally well in the RC model.

## 3.2  A model of rule competition

A central question for a theory of past tense formation, and consequently, for a theory of past tense acquisition, is the following: Should the *-d* rule be considered together with the inflection of the irregular as an integrated computational system, or should they be treated by using different modules of cognition? The approach advocated here is rooted in the first tradition, along the lines pursued in Chomsky & Halle (1968), Halle & Mohanan (1985), and the present-day Distributed Morphology (Halle & Marantz 1993).

These rules of verbal inflection constitute a continuum of productivity and generality that extends from affixation of the *-ed* suffix in *decide-decided* to total suppletion in *go-went....* In an intermediate class of cases exemplified by verbs like *sing-sang* or *bind-bound* the changes affect only a specific number of verbs. To deal with such cases, the grammar will not contain a plethora of statements such as 'the past tense of *sing* is *sang*, the past tense of *bind* is *bound*,' etc. Rather, it will contain a few rules, each of which determines the stem vowels of a list of verbs specifically marked to undergo the rule in question. (Halle & Mohanan 1985: 104)

This approach differs from the WR model, in which irregular verbs are individually memorized, to the effect of having 'a plethora of statements'.

### 3.2.1   A simple learning task

Before diving into the details of our model, let's consider a simple learning task, which may help the reader understand the core issues at a conceptual level.

Suppose one is asked to memorize the following sequences of pairs of numbers $(x, y)$:

(37)   (2, 4), (3, 4), (4, 8), (5, 10), (6, 7), (7, 8), (8, 16)

Obviously, one strategy to do this is to memorize all the pairs in (37) *by rote*. The learner will store in its memory a list of pairs, as is: (2, 4), (3, 4), etc. However, there is another strategy, which, when available, seems to be a more effective solution. Notice that (37) contains two regularities between the two paired numbers $(x, y)$ that can be formulated as two rules: $y = x + 1$ for {3, 6, 7} and $y = 2x$ for {2, 4, 5, 8}. In the memory of a learner that employs the second strategy, a list of *x*s will be associated with the rule that generates the corresponding *y*s:

(38)   a.   $\{3, 6, 7\} \mapsto R_{x+1}$
      b.   $\{2, 4, 5, 8\} \mapsto R_{2x}$

We liken the acquisition of irregular verbs to the number pair learning task described here. The WR model employs the first strategy: irregular verbs are memorized by rote as associated pairs such as *feed-fed, bring-brought, shoot-shot, think-thought*. The RC model, based on a system of generative phonological rules, employs the second strategy such that irregular verbs are organized by rules that apply to a class of individuals:

(39) a. {feed, shoot, ...} ↦ $R_{\text{Vowel Shortening}}$
b. {bring, think, ...} ↦ $R_{\text{-t suffixation \& Rime} \rightarrow a}$
c. ...

In an information-theoretic sense, the rule-based strategy, which allows a more 'compact' description of the data, is the more efficient one.[1] The present model is inspired by Morris Halle's idea (e.g. 1983, 1997a) that rules, and abstract representation of phonological structures in general, serve the purpose of saving storage space in the mental lexicon.

Furthermore, there is reason to believe that the rule-based strategy is preferred when verbs (rather than numbers) are involved. While the number-pairing rules can be arbitrary and mentally taxing, the rules for irregular verbs are not. Irregular past tense rules are often well-motivated phonological processes that are abundantly attested in the language. For example, the rule of Vowel Shortening[2] for verbs such *lose, feel,* and *say*, which shortens the long vowel in closed syllables followed by *-d*, *-ø*, and *-t* suffixes, is attested in many other suffixation processes in English. Therefore, such rules are frequently encountered by and naturally available to the learner.

With this conceptual background, let us move on to the RC model. In what follows, we will describe the properties of the phonological rules for past tense, and how they compete in the process of learning.

### 3.2.2 Rules

The past tense rules in English fall into two broad dimensions: suffixation and readjustment (Chomsky & Halle 1968, Halle

---

[1] While the saving achieved by the use of rules may not be significant for English irregular verbs—there are only some 150 in all—it becomes dramatic when we move to other languages. This, along with the issue of irregular phonology in other languages, will be discussed in section 3.4.

[2] The term 'Vowel Shortening' is perhaps a a misnomer. The change in the quality of the vowel actually involves shortening as well as lowering. While keeping this technical issue in mind, we will nevertheless continue to call such processes Vowel Shortening; see Myers (1987) and Halle (1998).

1990). Suffixation attaches one of the three past tense suffixes, *-d*, *-t*, and *-ø* (null morpheme),³ to the verb stem. Readjustment rules, mostly vowel-changing processes, further alter the phonological structure of the stem.

We assume, along with the WR model, that as part of innate Universal Grammar, the child language learner is equipped with the knowledge of a default rule, which applies when all else fails. The default rule for English verb past tense is given in (40):

(40)  *The default -d rule:*

$$x \xrightarrow{-d} x + \text{-d}$$

Irregular verbs fall into a number of *classes* as they undergo identical or similar suffixation and readjustment processes. Thus, verbs in a class are organized by a shared rule/process. Such a rule is schematically shown in (41), while the rule system for the most common irregular verbs is given in Appendix B.

(41)  *Rule R for verb class S:*

$$x \xrightarrow{R} y \text{ where } x \in s = \{x_1, x_2, x_3, \ldots\}$$

For example, the verb class consisting of *lose, deal, feel, keep, sleep*, etc. employs R = [*-t* Suffixation and Vowel Shortening] to form past tense. Suffixation and readjustment rules are generally independent of each other, and are in fact acquired separately. For example, the suffixes in derivational morphology such as *ity, -al*, and *-tion* must be acquired separately, but they all interact with Vowel Shortening, a readjustment rule that applies to closed syllables under many kinds of suffixation, as shown by Myers (1987):

(42)  Vowel Shortening in Suffixation
    a. [ay]–[ɪ]: divine-divinity
    b. [i]–[ɛ]: deep-depth
    c. [e]–[æ]: nation-national
    d. [o]–[a]: cone-conic
    e. [u]–[ʌ]: deduce-deduction

---

³ See Halle & Marantz (1993) for arguments that the -ø(null) morpheme is 'real'.

It is natural that pervasive rules like Vowel Shortening can be readily built in to the speaker's phonology, and can be used to form verb classes.[4]

Now the conceptual similarities and differences between the WR model and the RC model ought to be clear. It is not the case that the role of memory is completely dispensed with in the RC model. Every theory must have some memory component for irregular verbs: irregularity, by definition, is unpredictable and hence must be memorized, somehow. The difference lies in *how* they are memorized. In the WR model, irregular verbs and their past tense forms are stored as simple associated pairs, and learning is a matter of strengthening their connections. In the RC model, irregular verbs and their past tense forms are related by phonological rules (suffixation and readjustment), as schematically shown in Fig. 3.1.

Once a rule system such as (41) is situated in a model of learning, a number of important questions immediately arise:

(43)   a.  Where do rules such as suffixation and readjustment come from?
         b.  How does the learner determine the default rule (-*d*)?
         c.  How does the learner know which class a verb belongs to?
         d.  How do the rules apply to generate past tense verbs?

We postpone (43c) and (43d) until section 3.2.3, while (43a) and (43b) can be addressed together.

For our purposes, we will simply assume that the relevant rules for past tense formation, both the default and the irregular, are available to the child from very early on.[5] That is, the child is able to extract -*t*, -ø, and -*d* suffixes from past tense verbs, and can arrive at the appropriate sound-changing readjustment rules that

---

[4] Note that some irregular verbs are conventionally grouped into vowel shifting classes, e.g. ablaut and umlaut, that are not as homogeneous as the Vowel Shortening class. Ablaut and umlaut only designate the *direction* of vowel shifting, e.g. front → back, but leave other articulatory positions, e.g. [± high/low], unspecified. Hence, further refinement is required within these heterogeneous classes (see Appendix B). We will return to the issue of class homogeneity in section 3.4.

[5] In the WR model, it is assumed that the default -*d* rule is not available until a little before the child's third birthday (Pinker, 1995). In section 3.5.3, we show that there is little empirical evidence for this view.

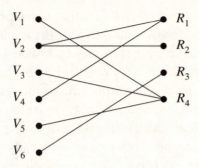

FIGURE 3.1. Verb and rule associations

relate the stem to the derived past tense form. The justification of our assumption is threefold.

First, our assumption is perfectly consistent with children's performance on the past tense. Recall that their past tense is very good (90% correct), and all their errors result from using a wrong rule: almost always the default, very rarely a wrong irregular rule. They do not produce random errors. This suggests that *knowledge* of the rules must be present. What remains problematic, as we shall show later on, is the *application* of these rules.

Second, there is strong crosslinguistic evidence that children's inflectional morphology is in general close to perfect; see Phillips (1995) for a review. For example, Guasti (1992) found that three young Italian children use agreement morphology correctly in more than 95% of all contexts. Clahsen & Penke (1992) had similar findings in a German child during the period of 1;7 to 2;8: the correct use of the affixes -*st* (2nd singular) and -*t* (3rd singular) is consistently above 90%. See Levy & Vainikka (1999) for comparable findings in Hebrew acquisition. And interestingly, when children's morphology occasionally deviates from adult forms, the errors are overwhelmingly of omission, i.e. the use of a default form, rather than substitution, i.e. the use of an incorrect form. This pattern is strikingly similar to that of English past tense learning, where overregularization is far more common than mis-irregularization (Xu & Pinker 1995). To acquire the inflectional morphologies in these languages, the learner must be able to extract the suffixes that correspond to the relevant syntactic/semantic features, and master the readjustment rules and processes when combining stems and suffixes. The learning procedure used there ought to carry over to English past tense.

Finally, recent work in computational modeling of phonological acquisition proposed by Yip & Sussman (1996, 1997) and extended by Molnar (2001) suggests not only that these rules can be learned very rapidly under psychologically plausible assumptions but that they are learnable by precisely the principle of storage minimization. Their system not only learns the correct past tense rules (regular and irregulars), but also learns the correct pluralization rules, at the same time. It learns with far greater efficiency and accuracy than every computational model proposed to date, including MacWhinney & Leinbach (1991), Ling & Marinov (1993), and Mooney & Califf (1995). Since this work is rather technical, we refer the reader to their original papers as well as expositions in Halle & Yang (2002) and Yang (2002).

The rapid learning of rules in the Yip–Sussman model is consistent with the observation that children's knowledge of inflectional morphology is virtually perfect. In section 3.2.3, we lay out the RC model that explains what remains problematic over an extended period of time: the application of these rules.

### 3.2.3 Rule competition

Class membership

We now return to question (43c), how children learn the class membership of irregular verbs. First, we assume, uncontroversially, that children are able to pair a root with its past tense: for example, when *sat* is heard, the learner is able to deduce from the meaning of the sentence that *sat* is the past tense realization of the root *sit*.[6] Once the root is extracted, the learner can proceed to associate it with the appropriate rule-based class.

---

[6] For a review that very young children can perform morphological analysis of word structures, see Clark (1993).

It is logically possible that children may put a verb into a wrong class. However, empirical evidence strongly speaks against this possibility. Again, the majority of past tense errors are overregularization errors, which on average occur in about 10% of all instances of irregular verbs (Marcus et al. 1992). Misapplication of irregular rules such as *bring-brang*, *trick-truck*, *wipe-wope*, dubbed 'weird past tense forms' by Xu & Pinker (1995), are exceedingly rare: about 0.2% (ibid.).[7] The rarity of weird past tense forms suggests that the child is conservative in learning verb class membership: without seeing evidence that a verb is irregular, the child generally assumes that it is regular, instead of postulating class membership arbitrarily.

Some notations before we proceed. Write $P(x \in S)$ for the probability that the learner correctly places $x$ into the verb class $S$. Also, write $f_x$ for the frequency of $x$ in past tense form in the input, and $f_S = \sum_{x \in S} f_x$ for the frequency of a verb *class*, which in the sum of the frequencies of all its members. These frequencies can be estimated from adult-to-child corpora such as CHILDES.

Learning by competition

We now turn to the central component of the RC model: how rules apply to generate past tense verbs, and consequently, how they model the learning behaviors in children's use of irregular verbs.

A central feature of the RC model is that rule application is not absolute. That is, every irregular rule $R$, which applies to the verb class $S$, is associated with a weight (or probability) $P_S$. For example, when the child tries to inflect *sing*, the irregular rule [-ø & ablaut], which would produce *sang*, may apply with a probability that might be less than 1. This follows if learning is gradual: it does not alter its grammar too radically upon the presentation of a single piece of linguistic evidence. If $R$ is probabilistically bypassed, the -$d$ rule applies as the default.[8]

---

[7] See Clahsen & Rothweiler (1993) for similar findings in German acquisition, and Saye & Clahsen (2002) for data in Italian acquisition.

[8] The present model should not be confused with a suggestion in Pinker & Prince (1988), which has an altogether different conception of 'competition'. Pinker & Prince

Now it should be obvious that we have departed from the Blocking Principle assumed in the WR model (Pinker 1995), also known the Elsewhere Condition (Kiparsky 1973) or the Subset Principle (Halle 1997b). The Blocking Principle states that when two rules or lexical items are available to realize a certain set of morphophonological features, the more specific one wins out. For example, *sang* is used to realize the past tense of *sing*, instead of *singed*, because the former is more specific than the latter default rule. Call this version of the Blocking Principle the Absolute Blocking Principle (ABP). In the present model, we suggest a stochastic version of the Blocking Principle (SBP): a more specific rule applies over the default rule *with a probability* (its weight). Thus, a more specific rule can be skipped in favor of a more general rule. The blocking effect of *sang* over *singed* in adult grammar indicates that the weight of the corresponding rule is 1 or very close to 1, *as a result of learning*. In section 3.2.4 we shall return to the Blocking Principle and give empirical arguments for our stochastic version.

An irregular rule $R$, defined over the verb class $S$, applies with probability $P_R$, once a member of $S$ is encountered. Thus, it competes with the default *-d* rule, which could apply to an irregular verb, and in fact does, when $R$ does not apply. The acquisition of irregular verb past tense proceeds as algorithm shown in Fig. 3.2.

Since regular verbs are almost never irregularized, i.e. the default *-d* rule is almost always employed, let us focus our attention on the case where the verb the learner encounters is an irregular one. When presented with a verb in past tense ($X_{past}$), the

---

suggest, much like the present model, that irregular verbs are dealt with by irregular rules (altogether this is not the position they eventually adopt). For them, the competition is *among* the irregular rules the learner postulates: e.g. rules $R_1$ and $R_4$ (the target rule) in Fig. 3.1 may compete to apply to the verb $V_1$. In the present model, the competition is between an irregular and *the default rule*. Under Pinker & Prince's suggestion, when the appropriate irregular rule loses out, another irregular rule will apply. This will result in the very rare mis-irregularization errors: the far more abundant overregularization errors, the main fact in the past tense problem, are not explained.

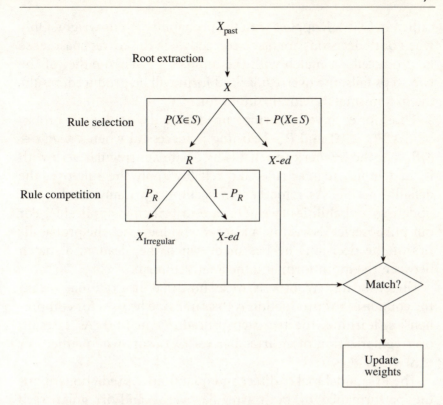

FIGURE 3.2. Learning irregular verbs by rule competition

learner first reconstructs the root $x$. As illustrated in Fig. 3.2, the learner then proceeds to analyze the derivation from $x$ to $X_{past}$ in a two-step process:

(44) a. Selection: associate $x$ to the corresponding class $S$ and hence the rule $R$ defined over this class.
b. Competition: apply to $R$ to $x$ over the default rule.

During learning, either of the two steps may be error-prone. First, the learner may not reliably associate $x$ to $S$, in which case $x$ would be treated as a regular verb (recall that it is virtually impossible for an irregular verb to be misclassified). That is, in (44a) the probability measure $P(x \in S)$ denotes the likelihood that the learner associates $x$ with $S$. Second, even if $x$'s class membership $S$ is correctly established, the corresponding rule $R$ may not apply:

rather, in (44b), $R$ applies with the probability $P_\mathcal{R}$, its weight. Only when both decisions are taken correctly will the correct past tense be produced—a match with the input $X_{past}$. When either of the two steps fails, the overregularized form will be produced, resulting in a mismatch with the input form, $X_{past}$.

Thus, for each verb, learning involves updating the two probabilities $P(x \in S)$ and $P_\mathcal{R}$. Learning is successful when $\forall x, P(x \in S)P_\mathcal{R} = 1$: the learner can reliably associate an irregular verb with its matching irregular rule, and reliably apply the rule over the default -$d$ rule. As remarked in section 2.3, many models for updating probabilities (weights) are in principle applicable. For our purpose, let us assume a learner who increases the probabilities of the decisions he has made when they lead to a match between the input form and the analyzed form.

Under the null hypothesis, we assume that the grammar system the child uses for production is the same one he uses for comprehension/learning, the two-step procedures in (44). As a result, overregularization of an irregular verb $x$ occurs when either $P(x \in S) < 1$ or $P_\mathcal{R} < 1$.

The RC model makes direct and quantitative predictions about the performance of both irregular verbs and irregular verb classes. Write $C(x)$ to denote the correct usage rate of an irregular verb $x$; clearly $C(x) = P(x \in S)P_\mathcal{R}$. While $P(x \in S)$ may increase when the past tense of $x$ is encountered, $P_\mathcal{R}$ may increases whenever *any* member of $S$ is encountered. These two probabilities, and hence the correct usage of an irregular verb $x$, is positively correlated with $f_x \times f_S$. Hence, if we hold $f_x$ or $f_S$ constant, the RC model makes two directions about the performance of irregular verbs:

(45) a. For two verbs $x_1$ and $x_2$ *within* a verb class, $C(x_1) > C(x_2)$ iff $f_{x1} > f_{x2}$.
    b. For two verbs $x_1$ and $x_2$ such that $x_1 \in S_1$, $x_2 \in S_2$, and $f_{x1} = f_{x2}$, $C(x_1) > C(x_2)$ iff $f_{S1} > f_{S2}$.

In section 3.3 we will systematically evaluate these predictions with children's production data, and demonstrate that irregular verbs are indeed organized into classes.

## 3.2.4 The Absolute and Stochastic Blocking Principles

We now give justifications for the Stochastic Blocking Principle (SBP), fundamental to the RC model.

Recall that in the WR model, the blocking effect of *sang* over *singed* is given by the ABP: *sang* is used because it is a more specific realization of *sing*+past. The ABP is central to the WR model: when it is presupposed, the rote memorization of irregular verbs is virtually forced. The fact is that children do overregularize, which should be impossible under the ABP. The WR model accounts for this by claiming that that irregular verbs are individually memorized. Overregularization errors are explained by appealing to a principle of association: more exposure leads to better memory. The memory imprints of irregular verbs in a child's mind are not as strong as those in an adult's mind, for children have not seen irregular verbs as many times as adults. Children overregularize because their memory retrieval has not yet become reliable.

Pinker (1995: 112) justifies the ABP by arguing that it is part of the innate endowment of linguistic knowledge, for it cannot be deduced from its effect. His reasoning is as follows. First, to learn the ABP, the child must somehow know that forms like *singed* are ungrammatical. Second, it cannot be concluded that *singed* is ungrammatical from its absence in adult speech—absence of evidence does not imply evidence for absence. Finally, Pinker claims that to know *singed* is ungrammatical 'is to use it and to be corrected, or to get some other negative feedback signals from adults like disapproval, a puzzled look, or a non sequitur response'. Since it is well established (e.g. Brown & Hanlon 1970, Wexler & Culicover 1980, Marcus 1993) that children do not have effective negative evidence, it is concluded that the ABP cannot be learned.

It is not the logic of this argument that we are not challenging; rather, it is the premise that the blocking effect of a more specific form over a more general form is absolute. We show that the effect of the blocking in adult language, the motivation for the Blocking Principle in the first place, can be duplicated as a result of learning, without negative evidence, under our stochastic version of the Blocking Principle.

Suppose that, initially, for the verb *sing*, the irregular rule $R=[-\emptyset$ & ablaut] and the default *-d* rule are undifferentiated. Upon presentation of the past tense form *sang*, both rules have a positive probability of being selected to realize *sing*+past. However, only when $R$ is selected can a match result, which in turn increases its weight (probability), $P_R$. In the end, $P_R$ becomes 1, so that *singed* will never be produced. The end product of such a competition process is a rule system that *appears* to obey the ABP but does not presuppose it: while the specific rule has priority—just as in the ABP—this preference is probabilistic, and gradually increases as a result of learning from experience. In the adult system, the default rule simply does not get a chance to apply, for the more specific irregular rule applies first, and with probability 1.

If the effect of the ABP can be duplicated by rule competition and statistical learning, its theoretical status needs to be reconsidered. Our second objection to the ABP is an empirical one. There is at least one good reason to reject the ABP: the presence of 'doublets'. For example, *learn*+past can be realized as either *learned* or *learnt*, *dive*+past can be realized as either *dived* or *dove*. For doublets, the ABP cannot be literally true, for otherwise *learned* and *dived* should never be possible, blocked by the more specific *learnt* and *dove*. However, the doublet phenomenon straightforwardly falls out of the SBP with a minor change to the learning algorithm: we suppose that the learner punishes $P_x$ when an expected irregular verb $x$ turns out to have regular forms. The term 'expected' is important here, implying that the learner has indeed seen irregular forms of $x$ before, but is now being confronted with conflicting evidence. Presumably, speakers that allow both *learned* and *learnt* encounter and use both forms.[9] As

---

[9] Including no less a literary genius than Lewis Carroll. In *Alice's Adventures in Wonderland*, *learnt* and *learned* appear exactly once each:

'Yes,' said Alice, 'we learned French and music.'

'Well, I can't show it you myself,' the Mock Turtle said: 'I'm too stiff. And the Gryphon never learnt it.'

a result of competition, the membership probability of *learn* in the corresponding irregular verb class will settle somewhere between 0 and 1, making alternating forms possible.

## 3.3 Words vs. rules in overregularization

In this section we examine children's overregularization data in detail. We show that the acquisition of irregular verbs shows strong class-based patterns, as predicted by the RC model and the rule-based approach to past tense in generative phonology.

### 3.3.1 The mechanics of the WR model

In order to contrast the RC model with the WR model, we must be explicit about how the WR model works and what predictions it makes. In the RC model, for any two irregular verbs, we have a concrete claim about their performance in children, based on their input frequencies and the collective frequencies of their respective classes (45), both of which can be estimated from corpora. It is not clear how predictions can be made with this level of clarity under the WR model. Since irregular verbs are learned by associative pairing in the WR model, it is crucial to have a precise statement of how such associative pairing is established. However, the closest to a clear statement that we can find in the WR literature is still vague:

It is not clear exactly what kind of associative memory fosters just the kinds of analogies that speakers are fond of. Possibly a network of word-word associations might give rise to the right generalization structure if the design of the lexical representation is informed by modern linguistic theory and its implementation is informed by models of superpositional memory. Here we can only present a rough sketch.

Words might be represented in a hierarchical hardware representation that separates stems and affixes, and furthermore distinguishes foot- and syllable-internal structure, finally representing segmental and featural composition at the lowest level of units. Furthermore each of the possible contents of each representation would be implemented once as a single hardware 'type'; particular words would be representation in separate 'token' units with pointers to the types it contains. Links between stems and pasts would be set up during learning between their representations at two levels:

between the token representations of each pair member, and their type representations at the level of representation that is ordinarily accessed by morphology: syllables, onsets, rhymes, feet (specifically, the structures manipulated in reduplicative and templatic systems, as shown in the ongoing work of McCarthy and Prince and others). Ordinary correct retrieval results from successful traversal of token-token links; this would exhaust the process for pairs like *go-went* but would be reinforced by type-type links for members of consistent and high-frequencies families like *sing-sang*. On occasions where token-token links are noisy or inaccessible and retrieval fails, the type-type links would yield an output that has some probability of being correct, and some probability of being an analogical extension (e.g., *brang*). Because the representation of input and output are each highly structured, such extensions would nonetheless be precise and follow constrained patterns, e.g., preserving portions of the stem such as onsets while substituting the appropriate rhymes, and avoiding the chimeras and fuzzy approximations that we do not see among real irregulars but that pure feature-to-feature networks are prone to making. (Pinker & Prince 1994: 334)

It is difficult to evaluate statements like these. The token level association is clear enough: the strength of brute force linking between a stem and its past, hence the retrieval rate of the corresponding verb, can be measured by estimating the frequency of the verb's occurrences in past tense. However, it is not clear how the type-level linkings between phonological structures (syllables, onsets, etc.) are established. But far worse is the vagueness concerning how the two levels interact. For example, while the token-level frequency effect is an important factor in past tense acquisition,[10] it is not clear when the type-level analogy becomes the operative force. Such imprecise formulations are not amenable to analytical results such as (45).

However, we believe that the evidence presented here is strong enough to rule out *any* model that does not use (irregular) phonological rules to describe irregular verbs. The data clearly point to an organization of irregular verbs by rules and classes.

---

[10] In fact, all 10 pieces of evidence offered by Pinker (1995) in support of the WR model, which we shall review in section 3.5, are frequency based, although section 3.3 has shown that frequency affects performance in a fairly subtle way, unexpected in the WR model.

## 3.3.2  The data

The measure of children's knowledge of irregular verbs is the correct usage rate (CUR), $C(x)$, defined as follows:

(46)  $C(x) = \dfrac{\text{total number of correct past tense of } x}{\text{total number of past tense of } x}$

Our data on child performance come from the monograph *Overregularization in Language Acquisition* (Marcus et al. 1992), where four American children (Adam 2;3–5;2, Eve 1;6–2;3, Sarah 2;3–5;1, and Abe 2;5–5;0) were studied, using the longitudinal recordings transcribed in the CHILDES corpus (MacWhinney & Snow 1985).[11] Marcus et al. manually analyzed the transcripts, and hence eliminated the unavoidable ambiguity that may have escaped computerized pattern extractions.[12] The input frequencies of irregular verbs are determined by the present author, based on more than 110,000 adult sentences to which Adam, Eve, Sarah, and Abe were exposed during the recording sessions.

The CURs of all irregular verbs, averaged over all recording sessions, are computed from Marcus et al. (1992: tables A1–A4) and given in (47):

(47) a.  Adam: 2446/2491 = 98.2%
     b.  Eve: 285/309 = 92.2%
     c.  Sarah: 1717/1780 = 96.5%
     d.  Abe: 1786/2350 = 76%

The average CUR for the four children is 89.9%. It is clear that there is quite a bit of individual variation among the children. While Adam, Eve, and Sarah used irregular verbs almost perfectly, Abe's performance is markedly worse. Of particular interest is the verb class [-ø & Rime → u], which includes verbs such as *know*, *grow*, *blow*, *fly*, and *throw*. This class posed significant difficulty

---

[11] Other children studied in the monograph are not included here, because of the relatively small size of their recordings and the lack of longitudinal data.

[12] For example, the past tense of no-change irregular verbs can only be accurately identified from the conversation context.

for all four children. The CURs are 7/16 = 44% (Adam), 0/1 = 0% (Eve), 12/22 = 55% (Sarah), and 28/71 = 39% (Abe). For Adam, Eve, and Sarah, this is the only seriously problematic class. We will explain this peculiar pattern in section 3.3.4.

The WR model learns and organizes irregular verbs on the principle of frequency-sensitive associative memory: the more you hear, the better you remember and the better you retrieve. Hence, $C(x)$ for the WR model is correlated with the frequency of $x$ in past tense form, $f_x$. In the RC model, the performance of an irregular verb $x$ is determined by two factors: the probability that $x$ is associated with its class $S$, and the probability $f_S$ of the rule $R$ applying over the default -$d$ rule. Hence, $C(x)$ in the RC model is correlated with $f_x \times \sum_{m \in S} f_m$.

## 3.3.3  Frequency hierarchy in verb classes

The first prediction made by the RC model is straightforward:

(48)  For two verbs $x_1$ and $x_2$ within a verb class, $C(x_1) > C(x_2)$ if $f_{x1} > f_{x2}$.

To test this prediction, we have listed some verbs grouped by class in (49), along with their input frequencies estimated from adult speech.[13] To make intra-class comparison, only non-trivial classes are included. Also, to minimize sampling effect, only verbs that were used by children at least twenty times are included in our study (Appendix C gives a complete list of irregular verbs with their frequencies):

(49)     *Verbs grouped by class*           *Input frequency*
    a.   [-*t* & Vowel Shortening]
         lose (80/82=97.6%)                 lost (63)
         leave (37/39=94.9%)                left (53)

---

[13] Past tense forms that can be unambiguously determined (e.g. *drew*, *took*) were counted by an automated computer search. Ambiguities that arise between past tense and present tense (e.g. *hit*), past participles (e.g. *brought*, *lost*), nouns (e.g. *shot*), and adjectives (e.g. *left*) were eliminated by manually combing through the sentences in which they occurred. Since we are comparing the relative CURs for verbs within a single class, no effort was made to distinguish past tense *put* and *got* from their participle forms, as it is clear that their frequencies thoroughly dominate other members in their respective classes.

b. [-t & Rime → a]
    catch (132/142=93.0%)      caught (36)
    think (119/137=86.9%)      thought (363)
    bring (30/36=83.3%)      brought (77)
    buy (38/46=82.6%)      bought (70)

c. [-ø & No Change]
    put (239/251=95.2%)      put (2,248)
    hit (79/87=90.8%)      hit (66)
    hurt (58/67=86.6%)      hurt (25)
    cut (32/45=71.1%)      cut (21)

d. [-ø & Vowel Shortening]
    shoot (45/48=93.8%)      shot (14)
    bite (33/37=89.2%)      bit (13)

e. [-ø & Backing ablaut]
    get (1269/1323=95.9%)      got (1,511)
    take (118/131=90.1%)      took (154)
    write (20/27=74.1%)      wrote (28)
    win (20/36=55.6%)      win (36)

f. [-ø & Rime → u]
    know (17/23=73.9%)      knew (49)
    throw (11/34=32.4%)      threw (28)

(49) strongly confirms the prediction in (48): within a single class, the more frequently a verb is heard, the better its CUR.[14] The 'exception' in class (49b), where *think*, a more frequent verb than *catch*, is used at a lower CUR, is only apparent. It is an averaging effect, as (50) makes clear:

(50) | Children | Verb | % correct |
|---|---|---|
| a. Adam, Eve, & Sarah | think | 100% (44/44) |
|  | catch | 96.5% (110/114) |
| b. Abe | think | 80.6% (75/93) |
|  | catch | 78.6% (22/28) |

The low averaged CUR of *think* in (49b) is due to a disproportionately large number of uses from Abe. Once individual variations are factored out as in (50), it is clear that *think* is used correctly at a higher frequency than *catch*, as predicted.

[14] The strong frequency–CUR correlation in the class [-ø & Backing ablaut] might not be taken at face value. The sound-changing patterns in this class are not homogeneous as in other classes, but are nevertheless conventionally labeled altogether as 'Backing ablaut'. See also n. 4.

(49) reveals a very important pattern: when verbs are grouped into classes defined by phonological rules, their performance is, virtually without exception, ordered by their input frequencies. This unequivocally points to the conclusion that irregular verbs are organized in (rule-defined) classes. This generalization cannot be stated in theories that do not have verb classes. In fact, the frequency–over-regularization correlation is also considered by Marcus et al. (1992: 118), who found that for the nineteen children tested, the correlation efficient is −0.37—significant, but far from perfect. What the WR model shows is that frequency plays an important role in the performance of irregular verbs; what it does not show is the precise manner in which frequency affects performance.

The frequency–performance correlation almost completely breaks down when verbs from *different* classes are considered. To see this, we turn to the second prediction made by the RC model, which reveals more empirical problems for the WR model.

### 3.3.4 *The free-rider effect*

Recall that the RC model predicts:

(51)   For two verbs $x_1$ and $x_2$ such that $x_1 \in S_1$, $x_2 \in S_2$ and $f_{x1} = f_{x2}$, $C(x_1) > C(x_2)$ if $f_{S_1} > f_{S_2}$.

(51) means that the CUR of an irregular verb $x$ could be quite high even if it is relatively infrequent, as long as other members of its class *S are* frequently encountered. This 'free ride' is made possible by the rule shared by all members of a class.

Since most high-frequency verbs are used correctly, we direct our attention to verbs in (49) that have the lowest input frequencies: *hurt* (25), *cut* (21), *bite* (13), and *shoot* (14). (We postpone the discussion of *bite* and *shoot* to section 3.3.5 for reasons that will become clear there.) We have also included *blew, grew, flew,* and *drew*, which appeared 5, 7, 14, and 22 times respectively, and belong to the [-ø & Rime → u] class that is problematic for all four children.

Consider the six irregular verbs in (52):

(52) Different performance with comparable frequencies (≤ 25 occurrences)
  Verb class              Verbs                  % correct
  a. [-ø & No Change]     hurt, cut              80.4% (90/112)
  b. [-ø & Rime → u]      draw, blow, grow, fly  35.2% (19/54)

Despite the comparable (and low) input frequencies, the verbs in (52a) and (52b) show a sharp contrast in CUR. This is mysterious under the WR model.

Furthermore, consider the asymmetry between *hurt* and *cut* with *know* and *throw*, the latter of which have considerably higher input frequencies than the former:

(53) Higher performance despite lower frequencies
  Verb class              Verb (frequency)       % correct
  a. [-ø & No Change]     hurt (25), cut (21)    80.4% (90/112)
  b. [-ø & Rime → u]      know (58), throw (31)  49.1% (28/57)

Here the verbs in (53a) are used better than those in (53b), despite their lower input frequencies. Again, it is not clear how the WR model accounts for this.

The asymmetries observed in (52) and (53) straightforwardly fall out of the RC model for a simple reason: the rule for (52a) and (53a) has much higher weights than those in (52b) and (53b), the free-rider effect. The first rule applies to the verbs *hurt* and *cut*, which do not change in past tense forms. The rule for this class, namely, [-ø & No Change], is amply represented in the input, including *hit, let, set, cut, put*, etc, which have very high usage frequencies, totaling over 3,000 occurrences. Every occurrence of such verbs increases the weight of the class rule. Hence, *hurt* and *cut* get a free ride, and have a high CUR despite a low absolute frequency. In contrast, verbs in (52b) belong to the [-ø & Rime → u] class (*blow, grow, know, throw, draw,* and *fly*), which totals only 125 occurrences in the input sample. Hence, the weight of the rule [-ø & Rime → u] must be considerably lower than that of [-ø & No Change]: the CUR asymmetry in (52) is thus accounted for.

A closer look at Abe's performance, which is markedly poor across all verb classes, reveals an even more troubling pattern for the WR model. Consider the verbs and their CURs in (54):

(54) Lower performance despite higher frequencies (Abe)

| Class | Verbs (frequency) | % correct |
|---|---|---|
| suppletion | go (567) | 0.646 (117/184) |
| [-ø & umlaut (∧ → ey)] | come (272) | 0.263 (20/76) |

The verbs in (54) are among the most common words in English and have far higher frequencies than those in (52a). However, for the low-frequency verbs in (52a), Abe has an average CUR of 0.659 (29/44, Marcus et al. 1992: table A8): in fact better than *went* and *came*.

This peculiarity in Abe's performance is readily explained by the RC model. Despite their relatively high frequencies, *go-went* and *come-came* nevertheless 'act alone', for they are in trivial classes. The suppletion case of *go-went* is obvious. *Come-came* belongs to the heterogeneous class [-ø & umlaut], which in fact consists of three subclasses with distinct sound changes: *fall* and *befall*, *hold* and *behold*, and *come* and *become*. Hence, *come* only receives help from *become*, which isn't much: two occurrences in all of the input.[15]

## 3.3.5 The effect of phonological regularity: Vowel Shortening

Consider the following two low-frequency verbs: *shoot* and *bite*, whose past tense forms appeared only 14 and 13 times respectively in more than 110,000 adult sentences. Nevertheless, they are used virtually perfectly—91.8% (78/85)—again in sharp contrast with the performance (40.5%) on the verbs in the [-ø & Rime → u] class (52b).

Past tense formation for both *shoot* and *bite* fall under the rule [-ø & Vowel Shortening]. As remarked in section 3.2.2 and in (42), Vowel Shortening is a pervasive feature of the English language. Furthermore, Myers (1987) and Halle (1998) show, from different

---

[15] Abe's performance on the other two umlaut subclasses are not much better: *fall-fell* is used correctly 72 times out of 129 uses, while *fell* appeared 279 times in the adult input, and *hold-held* is used correctly 0 of 4 times, while *held* appeared 11 times in the adult input, although the sample size in the latter case is too small to be truly informative.

perspectives, that Vowel Shortening is essentially free: vowels in closed syllables are automatically shortened under suffixation, resulting from the interaction between universal phonological constraints and language-specific syllabification properties. Given the evidence that (English) children have good grasp of the syllabic structure of their language (e.g. Smith 1973, Macken 1980), and that they perform morphological analysis of words from early on (Clark 1993), learning irregular verbs with Vowel Shortening is considerably simplified; in fact, reduced to learning which suffix (*-t*, *-ø*, or *-d*) is attached. And children are very good at learning suffixes, as we saw when reviewing their agreement morphology acquisition in section 3.2.2.

In (55), we see that all three classes of Vowel Shortening verbs have very high CURs:

(55) Vowel Shortening under suffixation

| | *Suffix* | *Verb (frequency)* | *% correct* |
|---|---|---|---|
| a. | [-t] | lose-lost (63) | 98% (80/82) |
| | | leave-left (53) | 95% (378/39) |
| b. | [-d] | say-said (544) | 99% (522/525) |
| c. | [-ø] | shoot-shot (14) | 94% (45/48) |
| | | bite-bit (13) | 90% (33/37) |

All verbs in (55) are used very well, almost irrespective of their individual frequencies, ranging from very frequent ones (*say-said*) to very rare ones (*shoot-shot*, *bite-bit*). Such complete frequency defiance, along with the asymmetries noted in (52), (52b), and (54), strongly point to the reality of class-defining phonological rules in the RC model.

## 3.4  Analogy, regularity, and rules

### 3.4.1  *The failure of analogy*

Section 3.3 has identified a major problem with the WR model. The regularity among verbs in a class, expressed in a shared phonological rule in the RC model, is not statable in the WR model.

Perhaps the notion of analogy, built on phonological similarity (of some sort), may duplicate the effect of rules without explicitly assuming them. This is the only way to account for the acquisition data where frequency–performance correlation breaks down. Consider Pinker's discussion on analogy:

> Analogy plays a clear role in language. Children, and adults, occasionally analogize the pattern in one regular verb to a new irregular verb (*write-wrote* → *bite-bote*). They also find it easier to memorize irregular verbs when they are similar to other irregular verbs. The analogizing is a hallmark of connectionist or parallel distributed processing associators; it suggests that human memory might be like a pattern associator. (Pinker 1995: 129)

As an example, Pinker goes on to suggest that rhyme may play a role in pattern association and memorization. For example, since *draw-drew, grow-grew, know-knew,* and *throw-threw* rhyme with each other, memorizing *draw-drew* facilitates the memorization of other irregular verbs, and vice versa. The *bite-bote* type error results from the occasional misuse of the rhyme analogy.

The alert reader might realize at this point that we have already seen empirical evidence that analogy by rhyme cannot be correct. In sections 3.3.4 and 3.3.5 we have compared children's performance on several low-frequency verbs. Of particular interest are verbs like *shoot-shot* and *bite-bit*, which were used very well, and verbs like *grow-grew* and *blow-blew*, which were used very poorly. However, note that the only irregular verb that *bite-bit* rhymes with is *light-lit*, which appeared only once in the more than 110,000 adult sentences sampled. Worse, *shoot-shot* does not rhyme with *any* irregular verb in English. If Pinker were correct in suggesting that rhyme helps irregular verb memorization, one would expect that *drew, grew, threw,* and *knew*, which rhyme with each other and thus help each other in memorization, would have *higher* retrieval success than *shot* and *bit*, which get help from no one. However, this is not the case.

Could some different forms of analogy (other than rhyme) work so that the WR model can be salvaged? One cannot answer this question unless a precise proposal is made. The question of how words are analogous to each other, and how analogy is actually used to facilitate learning, is usually left vague in the literature, under the rubric of the Wittgensteinian 'family resemblance' (e.g. Bybee & Slobin 1982, Bybee & Moder 1983, Pinker 1999). Here there is a methodological point to be made. While there is evidence that some human concepts cluster around fuzzy 'family resemblance' categories (Rosch 1978; but see Fodor 1998), rather than well-defined classical categories, there is no reason to suppose that the lexicon is organized in a similar way. Furthermore, the goal of modern cognitive science is to understand and model mental functions in precise terms. If one were to be content with vague ideas of analogy or association, such as the passage from Pinker & Prince (1994) quoted earlier, the systematic regularities among irregular verbs noted in section 3.3 will simply escape attention: they are revealed only under scrutiny of the empirical data guided by a concrete theoretical model proposed here.

Empirically, the 'fuzziness' in the use of past tense (Bybee & Slobin 1982, Bybee & Moder 1983) in no way shows that the organization of irregular verb phonology is built on 'prototypes' or 'analogy'. Rather, it simply reflects the probabilistic associations between words and rules, and the probabilistic competitions among rules, as the RC model demonstrates.

It seems that in order to capture the class-based frequency hierarchy reported in (49), the WR model must duplicate the class-defining effect of rules with 'analogy', the type-level association based on phonological similarities of verbs (in a class). But analogy works only when the sound similarities among verbs under identical rules/classes are strong enough *and* the sound similarities among verbs under different rules/classes are weak enough. A careful look at the irregular verbs in Appendix B shows this is highly unlikely. For example, verbs in the [-ø & No Change] class, such as *hit, slit, split, quit,* and *bid,* are very similar to those in the [–ø & Lowering ablaut] class, such as *sit* and *spit,* yet the two groups are distinct. Phonological similarity does not give a one-to-one mapping from verbs to classes, and that is why the traditional view in phonology (Chomsky & Halle 1968) treats verb and class association by fiat.

Or, consider the free-rider effect discussed in section 3.3.4, where phonological rules enable low-frequency verbs to be used with high accuracy. In order for the WR model to capture the free-rider effect with analogy, the 'family resemblance' among verbs of all frequencies must be very strong. This again leads one to expect that the learner will also strongly 'analogize' past tense formation to verbs that *do not* belong to the class but nevertheless *do* bear a superficial 'family resemblance' to the class members. For example, *think* may be analogized to *sing* and *ring* to yield *thank* or *thunk*. But children do not do this: about 0.2% in all verb uses are analogical errors (Xu & Pinker 1995).

Once we move beyond the impoverished morphology of English and on to other languages, it becomes immediately obvious that the use of phonological rules in the mental lexicon is inevitable. To take an example from Marcus et al. (1995), noun plurals in German employ five suffixes: *Kind-er* (children), *Wind-e* (winds), *Ochs-en* (oxen), *Daumen-ø* (thumbs; using an empty suffix like the English plural *moose-ø* and past tense *hit-ø*), and *Auto-s* (cars). The authors convincingly argue, using a sort of *Wug*-test with novel German nouns, that despite its low frequency, the -*s* is the default plural suffix, However, it is hard to imagine that German speakers memorize all four classes of irregular plurals—the majority of nouns in the language—on a word-by-word basis, as if each were entirely different from the others. It would also be a massive waste of memory.[16] Furthermore, it is the partial similarity among English irregular verbs that led Pinker and his colleagues to look for family resemblance:[17] four irregular classes of German noun plurals do not show any systematic similarity. Hence, no analogy comes to the rescue. It seems that German learners must sort each irregular noun into its proper class, as suggested by the traditional rule-based view.

---

[16] This inefficiency of memorization is not dramatic in English, a language with a very small irregular vocabulary.
[17] Which seems no more than a historical accident: see section 3.4.2.

The problem gets worse when we turn to languages with agglutinative morphology such as Turkish, or the so-called 'polysynthetic' languages (Baker 1996). These languages typically have very long 'words' built out of many morphemes, each of which expresses an individual meaning and all of which are glued together by both the morphophonological and the syntactic systems of the language. It is inconceivable that these 'words', which realize millions or billions of morphological feature combinations, are all individually memorized: some sort of combinatorial system must be employed.

This is not to say that analogy plays no role in learning. Mis-irregularization errors such as *bring-brang* in children and adults do seem analogy-based (Prasada & Pinker 1993).[18] However, the role analogy plays in learning must be highly marginal—precisely as marginal as the rarity of analogy errors, 0.2%. This suggests that a very weak effect of phonological analogy can be realized in the verb-to-class linking component of the RC model. As for an overall theory of past tense, it is important to realize, as Pinker & Prince (1988: 127, italics original) remark, that 'a theory that can *only* account for errorful or immature performance, with no account of why the errors are errors or how children mature into adults, is of limited value'. A model that banks on analogy, which can only explain weird past tense errors, misses the major target of the study.

### 3.4.2 Partial regularity and history

Before moving on, let us consider a major objection of proponents of the WR model to the rule-based approach. Since an irregular verb forms past tense by fiat, according to generative

---

[18] As pointed out to me by Noam Chomsky and Tom Roeper, by far the most frequent pattern in children's weird past tense errors involve verbs with an *-ing* ending such as *bring-brang* (Xu & Pinker 1995: table 2). In addition, *brang* is even acceptable to some speakers. Indeed, errors such as *bite-bote*, cited by Pinker (1995), and many conceivable errors (e.g. *think-thunk* after *sink-sunk*, *hit-hat* after *sit-sat*) were not found. This again suggests that analogy is a very weak influence.

phonology, there is no explanation why verbs like *sting, string, sling, stink, sink, swing,* and *spring* all change *i* to *u* in the past participle and all sound so similar (e.g. Pinker 1999: 102). Pinker's explanation is again based on family resemblance, the sort of fuzzy associations borrowed from connectionist networks. Since verbs are represented as bits and pieces of sound segments (Pinker & Prince 1994, Pinker 1999), the common parts they share are reinforced most often and thus become gravitational attraction for word families, with some prototypes close to the center such as *string-strung* and *sling-slung*, and some on the fringes such as *dig-dug* and *win-won*. But this reasoning seems circular: why are *these* verbs pulled into similarity-based families? As far as one can tell, because they sound similar. Also notice that stem similarity is only partial: the *i-u* family does not include *think*, whose past participle is *thought*, or *blink*, which is altogether regular, and both of them seem closer to the family center than *dig* and *win*. Nowhere does the WR model specify how fuzzy family resemblance actually works to prevent *thunk* and *blunk* from being formed.

The most important reason for this misguided challenge is, partial regularity in verb classes is a result of historical contingencies.

In the RC model, verb classes are defined by rules such as (41), repeated below:

(56) Rule R for verb class S

$x \xrightarrow{R} y$ where $x \in S = \{x_1, x_2, x_3, \ldots\}$

The members of $S$ are simply listed, and they share the $R$, which computes the output form, $y$. One can imagine another kind of rule that is defined in terms of *input*, where the past tense of the verb is entirely predictable from the stem:

(57) Rule R for verb class S

$x \xrightarrow{R} y$ where $x$ has property $\pi_S$

In present-day English, rules like (57) are full of exceptions, at least in the domain of the past tense. However, their regularities were higher further back in history. Even the suppletive verbs, which may seem arbitrary synchronically, are not necessarily accidents diachronically. In Middle English, for example, *go* somehow replaced the now obsolete *wend*. However, *go* did retain the past tense form, *went*, which belongs to the more regular class that also includes *bend* and *send*. Hence, the suffixation and readjustment rules, synchronically productive, are evidenced diachronically: no irregular verbs are exceptions to -*t*, -ø, and -*d* suffixation.

How did such (partial) regularities get lost in history? There are two main factors; see Pinker (1999: ch. 3) for a good discussion. One is purely frequency-based. If an irregular verb is used very infrequently, the learner will not reliably locate it in the appropriate class to which it belongs. We will return to this in section 3.5.9. The other factor falls out of the interaction between irregular rules and changes in other parts of the phonological system. See Pinker (1999: 65) for the history of the now archaic *wrought*. The evolution of irregular verbs is not completely random, therefore, but rather stochastic: sampling effects and other unpredictable changes, such as *go* replacing *went*, interact with predictable UG principles and conventions to produce partial similarities observed in irregular verb classes. The reader is referred to Yang (2002) for a formal model of sound change based on the RC model of learning, and for a detailed discussion of these issues.

## 3.5 Some purported evidence for the WR model

Pinker (1995) summarizes previous work on the WR model and gives ten arguments in its support. Here we review them one by one, and show that, where they are not factually inaccurate or methodologically flawed, they are handled equally well or better by the RC model.

### 3.5.1 Error rate
How low is it?
Pinker claims that the rate of past tense errors is quite low: the mean rate across twenty-five children is 4.2%, the median only

2.5%. He suggests that this low rate indicates that overregularization is 'the exception, not the rule, representing the occasional breakdown of a system that is built to suppress the error', as in the WR model.

First, it is questionable whether the actual error rate is actually *that* low. In (47), we saw that the error rate averaged over four children is 10.1%. In particular, Abe's error rate is *very* high: about 24% of the irregular verbs were regularized. Also, as is clear from Marcus et al. (1992: table A8), Abe's poor performance is systematic and cuts across all verb classes, and thus is not due to a few particularly bad and very frequent verbs/classes.[19] He even made a considerable number of errors (64/177=36%) in *go-goed*, while all other children used *went* perfectly throughout. Second, by averaging over all irregular verbs, the more problematic but less frequent verbs and classes and the important variations among classes (section 3.3) are lost. For example, all four children performed very badly on the [-ø & Rime → u] class, an error rate of 48.6% (54/111).

Longitudinal trends

Pinker claims that the rate of overregularization, 2.5%, is stable through the preschool years (2–5), and gives Adam's longitudinal overregularization trend, which is indeed quite steady (and low) over time. He concludes that the steady error rate is due to the occasional malfunction of memory retrieval—the exception, not the rule.

There are strong reasons to challenge this claim. First, it seems that Adam is the exception, rather than the rule. Adam's grasp of irregular verbs is in general perfect, the best among the four children we examined; see (47). Second, as already noted in section 3.5.1, averaging over all irregular verbs is likely to obscure longitudinal patterns, which could be observed only in problematic verbs (e.g. the *know-knew* class).

---

[19] See Maratsos (2000) for a discussion of Abe, in particular why the large set of data from Abe must be taken as seriously as those from other children.

Fortunately, we do have Abe, whose irregular verb performance is, across all verb classes, markedly worse than the other three children. To study Abe's longitudinal development, we have grouped every consecutive fifteen recordings into a period. There are 210 recordings (from 2;4 to 5;0), so we have fourteen periods altogether. We have examined verbs that Abe was particularly bad at: *go, eat, fall, think, came, catch, run,* and the members of the problematic [-ø & Rime → u] class: *throw, grow, know, draw, blow,* and *fly*. The results are are summarized in Table 3.1.

With the exception of period 1, in which Abe only had eighteen opportunities to overregularize (and there was thus a likely sampling effect), his error rate is gradually declining. This shows that children's overregularization at the earliest stage is considerably more significant and systematic than Pinker claims, and cannot be attributed simply to 'exception'.

## 3.5.2 *The role of input frequency*

Pinker notes that the more frequently an irregular verb is heard, the better the memory retrieval for that verb gets, and the lower the overregularization rate. This claim, while correct for verbs

TABLE 3.1. Abe's longitudinal overregularization for problematic verbs

| Period | No. of overregularization | Total no. used | Error rate |
| --- | --- | --- | --- |
| 1 | 3 | 18 | 0.167 |
| 2 | 14 | 25 | 0.560 |
| 3 | 31 | 50 | 0.620 |
| 4 | 27 | 37 | 0.729 |
| 5 | 10 | 19 | 0.526 |
| 6 | 28 | 56 | 0.500 |
| 7 | 28 | 54 | 0.519 |
| 8 | 7 | 38 | 0.184 |
| 9 | 18 | 52 | 0.346 |
| 10 | 10 | 40 | 0.250 |
| 11 | 4 | 33 | 0.121 |
| 12 | 4 | 23 | 0.174 |
| 13 | 2 | 43 | 0.047 |
| 14 | 3 | 46 | 0.065 |

within a class (section 3.3.3), is in general incorrect. The performance of an irregular verb is determined by two factors: the correct identification of class membership, and the weight of the irregular rule (see sections 3.3.4 and 3.3.5).

### 3.5.3 The postulation of the -d rule

In the stage which Pinker calls phase 1 (from 2;3 to shortly before 3;0), Adam left many regular verbs unmarked: instead of saying *Yesterday John walked*, the child would say *Yesterday John walk*. Overregularization started in phase 2, as the rate of tensed verbs very rapidly became much higher. Pinker suggests that the two phases are separated by the postulation of the *-d* rule. Although this appears to be a reasonable interpretation, it is problematic when individual variations and other aspects of language acquisition are taken into consideration.

First, individual variations. Pinker (1995) only gives the tendency of regular verb marking for Adam, based on Marcus et al. (1992: 109). However, on Marcus et al. (1992: 109–11) we see that the other three children showed very different patterns. Eve's use of regular verbs was basically in a steady climb from the outset (1;6). Sarah showed quite a bit of fluctuation early on, perhaps due to sampling effect, before gradually settling on an ascent. Abe, whose irregular verbs were marked poorly, nevertheless showed the highest rate of regular verb marking: he started out with about 70% of regular verb marking at 2;5, rising to 100% around 2;10.

Second, the low rate of tense marking in phase 1 may be complicated by the so-called Optional Infinitive (OI) stage, first reported by Weverink (1989). Children learning some but not all languages (including English) go through a stage in which they produce a large amount of nonfinite as well as finite verbs in matrix sentences as well as finite. Although there is no consensus on how OI should be explained, to the extent that the phenomenon is real, it may cause the lack of past tense marking.

Consider an alternative explanation of the rapid increase Pinker noted in the use of inflected verbs. No discontinuity in the

-*d* rule is supposed; that is, we assume that the -*d* rule is learned by the child quite early on, perhaps along the lines suggested by Yip & Sussman (1996, 1997). However, during the OI stage, the -*d* rule, which applies to past tense verbs, simply does not apply to the extensively used nonfinite verbs that are allowed by an OI stage competence system. When children leave the OI stage, the -*d* rule consequently becomes applicable.

A good test that may distinguish this position from Pinker's is to turn to a language for which the OI stage does not exist, so that OI is not a confounding factor. Italian and Spanish are such languages, where children reliably inflect verbs for tense (Guasti 1992, Wexler 1998). If the alternative view, that the -*d* rule is available from early on, is correct, we predict that in the acquisition of Italian and Spanish, irregular verbs ought to be overregularized from early on. The late postulation of the -*d* rule in the WR model does not make this prediction. So far we have not checked this prediction.

### 3.5.4 Gradual improvement

Pinker notes that after the -*d* rule is postulated (but see the previous section for an alternative view), overregularization does not drive out correct use of irregular verbs, but bare forms instead, which are extensively used during phase 1. He cites Adam's performance for support. Adam's average CUR is 0.74 during phase 1, and 0.89 during phase 2. There appears to be no 'real regression, backsliding, or radical reorganization' (1995: 118) in Adam's irregular verb use. This follows if the memory for irregular verbs is getting better.[20]

Gradual improvement is also predicted by the RC model, as weights for class membership and irregular rules can only increase. The gradual improvement in the performance results from the increasing amount of exposure to irregular verbs.

---

[20] The gradual improvement in Adam's performance seems to contradict Pinker's earlier claim that Adam's error rate is stable (section 3.5.1).

### 3.5.5 Children's judgement

Experiments have been conducted to test children's knowledge of irregular verbs, by presenting them with overregularized verbs and asking them if they sound 'silly'. Children are found to call overregularized verbs silly at above chance level. This finding is claimed to show that children's grammar does judge overregularization as wrong, despite their occasional use of it.

Pinker correctly points out some caveats with such experiments: a child's response might be affected by many factors, and thus is not very reliable. In any case, these findings are hardly surprising: even Abe, the child with by far the worse irregular verb use, had an overall error rate of 24%—far better than chance. In fact, such findings are compatible with any model in which children produce more correct forms than overregularizations at the time when judgements were elicited.

### 3.5.6 Anecdotal evidence

Pinker cites two dialogues (one is given below) between psycholinguists and their children, during which the adults use overregularized verbs to observe the children's reaction. The children are not amused.

*Parent*: Where's Mommy?
*Child*: Mommy goed to the store.
*Parent*: Mommy goed to the store?
*Child*: NO! (*annoyed*) Daddy, *I* say it that way, not you.

Pinker (1995: 119) suggests that the children, 'at some level in their minds, compute that overregularizations are ungrammatical even if they sometimes use them themselves'.

Whether anecdotal evidence should be taken seriously is of course a concern. Possibly, children do not like to be imitated. In any case, the RC model gives a more direct explanation for observed reactions. Recall that at the presentation of each past verb, the child has probabilistic access to either the special irregular rule (when applicable) or the default *-d* rule, to generate the expected past tense form from the extracted root. Now if an overregularized form such as *goed* is repeated several times, the chance of a mismatch (i.e. the child generating *went*) is consequently enhanced—the probability of generating *went* at least once in several consecutive tries—much to children's annoyance, it appears.

### 3.5.7 Adult overregularization

Adult do occasionally overregularize. Pinker claims that the rarity entails that adult overregularization is the result of performance, not the result of a grammatical system. However, this is not the only interpretation of adult overregularization: rule-based grammatical system approaches account for the data equally well. Under the RC model, for an irregular verb (e.g. *smite-smote*) that appears very sparsely, the learner may not be sure which class it belongs to, i.e. the probability of class membership association is considerably below 1. Overregularization thus results, even if the weight of the irregular rule for its corresponding class is very close to 1.

Pinker also notes that since memory fades when people get older, more overregularization patterns have been observed during experiments with older people (Ullman et al. 1993). This interesting finding is consistent with every theory that treats the irregulars as different—cognitively, and ultimately neurologically—from the regulars: in the RC model, it is the class membership that is memorized.

### 3.5.8 Indecisive verbs

Adults are unsure about the past tense of certain verbs that they hear infrequently. *Dreamed* or *dreamt*? *Dived* or *dove*? *Leapt* or *leaped*? *Strided* or *strode*?[21]

---

[21] Some of those forms are doublets, so both forms are heard. As noted in section 3.2.4, they pose a problem for the Absolute Blocking Principle, which the WR model adopts.

Pinker links input frequency to the success of irregular past tense (memory imprint). Again, this correlation is also expected under the RC model: low-frequency verbs give the learner little clue about class membership, and for doublets, the class membership is blurred by the non-trivial frequencies of both forms.

### 3.5.9 *Irregulars over time*

Pinker cites Joan Bybee's work showing that, of the 33 irregular verbs during the time of Old English, 15 are still irregular in Modern English, with the other 18 lost to the +*ed* rule. The surviving ones had a frequency of 515 uses per million (137/million in past tense), and the regularized ones had a frequency of 21 uses per million (5/million in past tense). The more frequently used irregulars are retained.

The RC model readily accounts for this observation. Suppose that for generation $n$, all 33 irregular verbs had irregular past tense forms, but some of them are very infrequently used. As a result, generation $n + 1$ will be unsure about the class membership of the infrequent irregulars, for reasons discussed in section 3.5.8, and will regularize them sometimes. Consequently, generation $n + 2$ will be even less sure and will produce more regularized forms. Eventually, when the irregular forms drop into nonexistence, such verbs will have lost their irregular past tense forever. Thus, the loss of irregularity is a result of sampling effects and competition learning over time. See Yang (2002) for a model that formalizes this process.

### 3.5.10 *Corpus statistics*

Based on the statistics from modern English text corpora, Pinker found that the top ten most frequently used verbs are all irregular verbs, and that 982 of the 1,000 least frequently used are regular verbs. He reasons that this pattern is predicted, since the survival of irregular verbs against children and adults' overregularization is only ensured by high frequency of use. This is certainly correct, but is also obviously compatible with the RC model, following the discussion in 3.5.8 and 3.5.9.

## 3.6 Conclusion

We have proposed a rule competition model for the acquisition of past tense in English. A list of irregular rules, defined over classes of irregular verbs, compete with the default *-d* rule for past tense inflection. Hence, the learning of an irregular verb is determined by the probability with which the verb is associated with the corresponding irregular rule, as well as the probability of the rule applying over the default *-d* rule. We have also given justifications for, and explored the consequences of, a stochastic and learning-theoretic version of the Blocking Principle.

The RC model is completely general, and applicable to the acquisition of phonology in other languages. Complemented by the Yip–Sussman model of rule learning, our model makes very precise predictions about verb learning: any two verbs can be directly compared (45), based on quantifiable frequency measures drawn from linguistic corpora. Such quantitative predictions are strongly confirmed by the acquisition data. We view the findings here as a strong challenge to any phonological theory that rejects rules.

Scrutiny over past tense 'errors' revealed much about the organization and learning of phonology. In Chapter 4, we turn to their syntactic counterparts.

## Appendix B: The rule system for English past tense

This list is loosely based on Halle & Mohanan (1985: appendix) and Pinker & Prince (1988: appendix). Very rare verbs are not listed.

## Suppletion

go, be

## -t suffixation

- No Change
 burn, learn, dwell, spell, smell, spill, spoil
- Deletion
 bent, send, spend, lent, build
- Vowel Shortening
 lose, deal, feel, kneel, mean, dream, keep, leap, sleep, leave
- Rime → a
 buy, bring, catch, seek, teach, think

## -ø suffixation

- No Change
 hit, slit, split, quit, spit, bid, rid, forbid, spread, wed, let, set, upset, wet, cut, shut, put, burst, cast, cost, thrust, hurt
- Vowel Shortening
 bleed, breed, feed, lead, read, plead, meet

## -d suffixation

- Vowel Shortening
 flee, say
- Consonant
 have, make
- ablaut
 sell, tell
- No Change (default)
 regular verbs

# Appendix C: Overregularization errors in children

Irregular verbs are listed by classes; in the text, only verbs with 25 or more occurrences are listed. The counts are averaged over four children. All raw counts from Marcus et al. (1992).

- [-t & Vowel Shortening]
  *lose* 80/82, *feel* 5/18, *mean* 4/5, *keep* 2/2, *sleep* 3/6, *leave* 37/39
- [-t & Rime → a]
  *buy* 38/46, *bring* 30/36, *catch* 132/142, *teach* 8/9, *think* 119/137
- [-ø & No Change]
  *hide, slide, bite, light*
  *shoot*
- Lowering ablaut
  *sit, spit, drink, begin, ring, shrink, sing, sink, spring, swim*
  *eat, lie*
  *choose*
- Backing ablaut
  I → ∧    *fling, sling, sting, string, stick, dig, win*
  ay → aw  *bind, find, grind, wind*
  ay → ow  *rise, arise, write, ride, drive, strive, dive*
  ey → u   *take, shake*
  er → or  *bear, swear, tear, wear*
  iy → ow  *freeze, speak, steal, weave*
  ε → a    *get, forget*
- umlaut
  *fall, befall*
  *hold, behold*
  *come, become*
- Vowel → u
  *blow, grow, know, throw, draw, withdraw, fly, slay*
  *hit* 79/87, *cut* 32/45, *shut* 4/4, *put* 239/251, *hurt* 58/67
- [-ø & Vowel Shortening]
  *feed* 0/1, *read* 1/2, *hide* 4/5, *bite* 33/37, *shoot* 45/48
- [-ø & Lowering ablaut]
  *sing* 3/4, *drink* 9/15, *swim* 0/3, *sit* 5/7, *spit* 0/3
  *eat* 117/137
- [-ø & Backing ablaut]
  *stick* 5/10, *dig* 2/5, *win* 20/36
  *ride* 7/8, *drive* 6/12
  *take* 118/131, *shake* 4/4
  *get* 1269/1323, *forget* 142/142

- [-ø & umlaut]
  *fall* 266/334
  *hold* 0/5
  *come* 109/174
- [-ø & Rime → u]
  *blow* 5/15, *grow* 4/12, *know* 17/23, *throw* 11/34, *draw* 2/12, *fly* 8/15
- [-d & Vowel Shortening]
  *say* 522/525

# 4

# Grammar Competition in Children's Syntax

> Phylogenesis is the mechanical cause of ontogenesis. The connection between them is not of an external or superficial, but of a profound, intrinsic, and causal nature.
> Ernst Hackel, *Ontogeny and Phylogeny* (Gould 1977: 78)

Hackel's proposition that 'ontogeny recapitulates phylogeny', which has been drifting in and out of fashion in biology, may well be vindicated in the ontogeny of human language, with a twist. If language is delimited in the finite space of Universal Grammar, its ontogeny might well recapitulate its scope and variations as the child gradually settles on one out of the many possibilities. This is exactly what the variational model leads one to expect, and the present chapter documents evidence to this end.

The variational model also serves another important purpose. If we survey the field of language acquisition, we cannot fail to notice an unfortunate gap between learnability studies and developmental studies. As far as we know, there is presently no formal model that directly explains developmental findings, nor any rigorous proposal of how the child attains and traverses 'stages' described in developmental literature. The variational model intends to fill this gap.

The variational model makes two general predictions about child language development:

(58) a. Other things being equal, the rate of development is determined by the penalty probabilities of competing grammars; cf. (25).
b. As the target grammar gradually rises to dominance, the child entertains coexisting grammars, which ought to be reflected in the non-uniformity and inconsistency in its language.

What follows is a preliminary investigation of (58) through several case studies in children's syntactic development.[1] These cases are selected for two reasons. First, they are based on a large body of carefully documented quantitative data.[2] Second, they are major problems in acquisition that have received a good deal of attention. Nevertheless, we will show that some interesting and important patterns in the data have never been noticed; in addition, an explanation of them may not be possible unless a variational approach is assumed.

This chapter is organized as follows. Section 4.1 presents crosslinguistic longitudinal evidence in support of prediction (58a), drawing evidence from child French, English, and Dutch. The statistics established there will be used in section 4.2 in a quantitative interpretation of the Argument from the Poverty of Stimulus presented in response to recent challenges by Sampson (1989) and Pullum (1996). Section 4.3 gives a systematic account of null subjects in child English, in comparison with child Chinese and Italian. Based on the children's null subject *Wh* questions and null object sentences, we show that English children have simultaneous access both to an obligatory subject grammar (the target) and to an optional subject grammar, supporting prediction (58b). The case studies will be concluded with a 'working manual' for acquisition studies in the variational framework.

## 4.1 Learning three parameters

Recall that from (25), we know that the penalty probability of the competitor grammar (or parameter value) determines the rate of language (or parameter) learning. Following the discussion of parameter learning in section 2.4, we estimate the frequency of signatures that unambiguously express the target value of each of three parameters under study. We will test the variational model

---

[1] Section 4.2 represents joint work with Julie Anne Legate; for a different and fuller treatment, see Legate & Yang (in press).
[2] Hence a large debt is due to the researchers who collected the data used here.

by examining the acquisition of three parameters: that of finite verb raising in French (Pierce 1989), acquired early, that of obligatory subject use in English (Valian 1991, Wang et al. 1992), acquired relatively late, and that of V2 in Dutch (Haegeman 1995), also acquired late.

Before moving on, we would like to clarify our claim here that some parameters are acquired later than others. As reviewed in section 2.1, the dominant view, shared by researchers from a wide spectrum of theoretical inclinations, is that parameters are set correctly from early on: for the subject parameter, see e.g. Bloom (1990, 1993), Valian (1991), Hyams (1996), Wexler (1998), and for the V2 parameter, see e.g. Boser (1992) and Poeppel & Wexler (1993). While we believe that the setting of the verb-raising parameter, and indeed of many parameters, is genuinely early, the claim that the subject and the V2 parameters are also set early is unconvincing. As we shall see shortly, for some parameters, assertions of early setting either fail to explain important developmental patterns or amount to dismissing up to half of the quantitative data.

## 4.1.1 *Verb raising and subject drop: the baselines*

Consider first the verb to Tense raising parameter, for which the [+] value is expressed by signature of the type $V_{FIN}$ Neg/Adv. A grammar with the [−] value for this parameter is incompatible with such sentences; when probabilistically selected by the learner, the grammar will be punished as a result. Based on the CHILDES corpus, we estimate that such sentences constitute 7% of all French sentences heard by children. Since verb raising in French is an early acquisition, by 1;8 (Pierce 1989; for similar findings in other verb-raising languages, see Wexler 1994), this suggests that 7% of unambiguous signatures—an entirely *post hoc* figure—is a lower bound that suffices for an early acquisition: any aspect of grammar with at least 7% of signatures should also be acquired very early.

We then have a direct explanation of the well-known observation that word order errors are 'triflingly few' (Brown 1973: 156) in children acquiring fixed word order languages. For example, English children rarely produce word orders other than SV/VO, nor do they fail to front *Wh* words in questions (Stromswold 1990). Observe that virtually all English sentences display rigid word order, e.g. verb almost always (immediately) precedes object. Also, *Wh* words are almost always fronted in questions, which, in our estimation, constitute roughly one third of all sentences English children hear. These patterns give a very high (far greater than 7%) rate of unambiguous signatures, which suffices to drive out other word orders very early on.

From (58a) it also follows that if signatures are rare in the input, the development of a grammar (or a parameter) will be relatively late. Consider then the acquisition of subject use in English. Following Hyams (1986), Jaeggli & Safir (1989), and many others, the use of pure expletive (*there*) subjects (59) correlates with the obligatoriness of subject use in a language:

(59)  a. There is a man in the room.
      b. Are there toys on the floor?

Optional subject languages do not have to fill the subject position, and therefore do not need placeholder items such as *there*.[3] We estimate that expletive sentences constitute 1.2% of all adult sentences to children, based on the CHILDES database. Subject use is acquired relatively late—at 3;0 (Valian 1991), judged by comparability with adult usage frequency[4]—we may conclude

---

[3] This does not mean that we are committed to a particular parameter, [± pro-drop] or [± Null Subject], which is in any case too crude to capture the distributional differences between two representative classes of optional subject grammars, the Italian type and the Chinese type. We only make the assumption that languages make a small number of choices with respect to the use of subject. We are, however, committed to what seems to be a correct generalization that the use of expletive subjects and the obligatoriness of subject are correlated—hence, something in UG must be responsible for this.

[4] As remarked earlier, Valian nevertheless claims that the subject parameter is set correctly, and attributes the missing subjects to performance limitations; we will return to this in section 4.3.2.

that 1.2% of unambiguous evidence ought to result in a late acquisition. Similar to the case of French verb raising, we will use 1.2% as a baseline for *late* acquisition: if a parameter is expressed by 1.2% of the input, then its target value should be set relatively late; more specifically, as late as the consistent use of subjects in child English.

### 4.1.2  V1 in V2 learners

Consider then the acquisition of the V2 parameter in Dutch. As noted in (26), there appears to be no direct signature for the V2 parameter: the four competitor grammars together provide a complete covering of the V2 expressions. However, three competitors, namely, the English, Irish, and Hixkaryana type grammars, while compatible with SVO, XVSO, and OVS patterns respectively, nevertheless have very high penalty probabilities: 35.3%, 66%, and 98.7%, according to our corpus analysis. As a result, these grammars are eliminated quite early on; see Fig. 2.1.

A Hebrew grammar, or a similar Semitic grammar such as Arabic, fares considerably better in the competition. By the virtue of allowing SVO and XVSO alternations (Fassi-Fehri 1993, Shlonsky 1997), it is compatible with an overwhelming majority of V2 patterns (98.7% in all). However, it is not compatible with OVS sentences, which therefore are in effect unambiguous signatures for the target V2 parameter after the other three competitors have been eliminated very rapidly. The rarity of OVS sentences (1.3%) implies that the V2 grammar is a relatively late acquisition, with a Hebrew-type non-V2 grammar in coexistence with the target V2 grammar for an extended period of time.

A Hebrew type grammar, then, allows verb-initial (V1) sentences, which are ungrammatical for the target V2 grammar, but will nevertheless constitute a significant portion of Dutch child language, if the variational model is correct. This prediction is confirmed based on the statistics from a Dutch child, Hein

(Haegeman 1995), one of the largest longitudinal studies in the acquisition of V2 languages.[5] The data concern the position of the finite verb in matrix sentences, and are reported in Haegeman's tables 5 and 6, which we combine in Table 4.1.

Based on these, we can compute the ratio of V1 sentences over all sentences. The number of V1 sentences is the number of postverbal subject sentences minus those with overt material left of V; that is, column 3 minus column 2 in Table 4.1. The number of all sentences is the sum of column 2 and column 3 in Table 4.1. The results are shown in Table 4.2.

Some of the V1 patterns are given below (from Haegeman 1995: n. 21):

(60) a. Week ik neit.
       know I not
   b. Zie ik nog niet.
       see I yet not
   c. Schijnt de zon.
       shines the sun
   d. Kan ik niet lopen.
       can I not run

Now we have to be sure the V1 patterns in (60) are 'real', i.e. are indeed due to the presence of a competing Semitic-type grammar. First, it must be stressed that all the sentences contain overt subjects, hence ruling out the possibility that the superficial V1 patterns are due to subject drop, which Germanic children are known to use. Another compounding factor is the precise location of the (finite) verb. According to Shlonsky (1997), finite verbs in Hebrew move to a position above Tense, presumably an Agreement node. Thus, if the V1 patterns are genuinely Hebrew-like, the finite verb must reside in a position higher than Tense. The presence of an overt subject again confirms this. Stromswold & Zimmerman's (1999) large quantitative study shows, contrary to the earlier claims of Deprez & Pierce (1993), that the subject is consistently placed above Negation,

---

[5] I should point out that Haegeman's paper does not directly deal with the V2 phenomenon, but with the nature of Optional Infinitives instead; it happens to contain a large body of quantitative data needed by our study.

TABLE 4.1. Subjects and non-subject topics in Hein's finite clause

| Age | Preverbal subject | Postverbal subject | Overt material left of V |
|---|---|---|---|
| 2;4 | 76 | 94 | 22 |
| 2;5 | 44 | 88 | 22 |
| 2;6 | 239 | 172 | 25 |
| 2;7 | 85 | 116 | 23 |
| 2;8 | 149 | 143 | 49 |
| 2;9 | 126 | 143 | 55 |
| 2;10 | 146 | 175 | 82 |
| 2;11 | 124 | 135 | 99 |
| 3;0 | 126 | 120 | 64 |
| 3;1 | 108 | 160 | 59 |

TABLE 4.2. Hein's longitudinal V1 patterns

| Age | V1 sentences | All sentences | % of V1 sentences |
|---|---|---|---|
| 2;4 | 72 | 170 | 43 |
| 2;5 | 66 | 132 | 50 |
| 2;6 | 147 | 411 | 36 |
| 2;7 | 93 | 201 | 46 |
| 2;8 | 94 | 292 | 32 |
| 2;9 | 98 | 269 | 36 |
| 2;10 | 93 | 321 | 28 |
| 2;11 | 36 | 159 | 14 |
| 3;0 | 56 | 246 | 22 |
| 3;1 | 101 | 268 | 37 |

presumably in the [Spec, T] position. Hence, the verbs in (60) are higher than Tense, consistent with the Hebrew-type grammar.

From Table 4.2, we see that before 2;6 the child used V1 patterns in close to 50% of all sentences; see Wijnen (1999) for similar findings. It thus disconfirms the claim that the V2 parameter is set correctly very early (Poeppel & Wexler 1993, Wexler 1998). With half of the data showing V1 patterns, to say that children have learned V2, or have adult-like grammatical competence, is no different from saying that children use V2 randomly.[6]

---

[6] One may object that the V1 patterns are due to the process of topic drop, and thus maintain the early setting of the V2 parameter. But this only begs the question: how do Dutch children figure out that topic drop is not used in their language? And there would still be half of the data to explain away.

Before we move on, consider the influential paper by Poeppel & Wexler (1993) in which the claim of early V2 setting is made. They found that in child German, while nonfinite verbs overwhelmingly appear in the final (and not second) position, finite verbs overwhelmingly appear in the second (and not final) position. But this does not warrant their conclusion that the V2 parameter has been set. A finite verb in the second position does not mean it has moved to the 'V2' position, particularly if the preverbal position is filled with a subject, as some of the examples taken from Poeppel & Wexler (1993: 3–4) illustrate below:

(61)   a.   Ich hab ein dossen Ball.
            I   have a big     ball
       b.   Ich mach das nich.
            I   do    that not

If this were true, then an English utterance like *Russell loves Mummy* would be classified as a V2 sentence. Poeppel & Wexler's data do show, however, that finite verbs raise to a higher position and nonfinite verbs stay in the base position, thus replicating Pierce's (1989) French findings in child German.

As shown in Table 4.2, Hein's use of V1 sentences dropped to about 14–20% at 3;0.[7] This can be interpreted as the target V2 grammar gradually wiping out the Hebrew-type grammar. Furthermore, because the frequency (1.3%) of Dutch OVS sentences is comparable to the frequency (1.2%) of English expletive sentences, we predict, on the basis of (25) (see Chapter 2), that the V2 parameter should be successfully acquired at roughly the same time that English children have adult-level subject use—3;0. If we use Brown's criterion that 90% correct usage signals successful acquisition, we may conclude that the Dutch child studied by Haegeman has mastered V2 at 3;0, or has come very close. There is also evidence from the acquisition of German, a similar language, that children reach adult-level V2 use by 3;0–3;3

---

[7] We suspect the unexpectedly higher rate of V1 at 3;1 to be a sampling effect: while all stages were recorded over 5–10 sessions, the recording at 3;1 took place in only one session.

(Clahsen 1986). Under the present model, it is no coincidence that the timing of the acquisition of English subject use and that of Dutch/German V2 are comparable.

## 4.2 Quantifying the stimulus poverty argument

Based on the acquisition model and the findings in section 4.1, we can give a quantitative evaluation of the Argument from the Poverty of Stimulus (APS).

Recall from section 1.1 that at the heart of APS lies the question: why do human children unequivocally settle on the correct (structure-dependent) rules for question formation, while the input evidence does not rule out the incorrect, structure-independent, inductive generalization?

(62) a. Front the first auxiliary verb in the sentence.
 b Front the auxiliary verb that is most closely follows a noun.
 c. Front the last auxiliary verb in the sentence.
 d. Front the auxiliary verb whose position in the sentence is a prime number.
 e. ...

for which the relevant evidence is in many ways ambiguous:

(63) a. Is Alex *e* singing a song?
 b. Has Robin *e* finished reading?

Recently, the argument for innate knowledge based on structure dependency has been challenged by Sampson (1989), Pullum (1996), and Cowie (1998), among others. They claim that the learner is actually exposed to the relevant evidence to rule out the incorrect, structure-independent hypotheses. Here we will focus on Pullum's objections and show that they are not valid.

First, Pullum (implicitly) assumes that there is only *one* alternative hypothesis to be ruled out, namely, that of (62a), the inversion of the first auxiliary in the sentence. This assumption is incorrect: the learner in fact has to rule out *all*, in principle infinitely many, hypotheses compatible with (63); cf. Freidin (1989). But for the sake of argument, suppose it were the case that the

110  *Competing Grammars*

learner had only a binary choice to make, while keeping in mind that if the learner did not have prior knowledge of structure dependency, the effort it takes to rule out all possible hypotheses can only be harder than that to rule out just (62a).

Second, Pullum notes, correctly, that auxiliary inversion in *yes/no* questions is not the only type of sentences that rules out (62):

(64)   Is$_2$ [the boy who is]$_{NP}t_1$ in the corner smiling?

*Wh* questions with an inverted auxiliary over a complex NP are also informative:

(65)   How could$_1$ [anyone that was awake]$_{NP}t_1$ not hear that?

Pullum proceeds to count the frequency of sentences such as (64) and (65), using a *Wall Street Journal* corpus. He discovered that in the first 500 sentences he examined, 5, or 1%, are of these two types. Some examples are given below:

(66)   a.   How fundamental are the changes these events portend?
       b.   Is what I'm doing in the shareholders' best interest?
       c.   Is a young professional who lives in a bachelor condo as much a part of the middle class as a family in the suburbs?
       d.   Why did 'The Cosby Show's' Lisa Bonet, who has a very strong screen presence, think that participating in a graphic sex scene would enhance her career as a legitimate actress?

Pullum then concludes that the APS is flawed, since the learner does have access to a non-trivial amount of disambiguating evidence.

This argument commits a logical error: a mere demonstration that critical evidence exists does not mean that such evidence is *sufficient*. Knowledge despite insufficiency—rather than absence—of relevant learning experience is the foundation of the APS.

It then forces us to the problem of how to quantify 'sufficiency' of critical evidence that serves to disambiguate alternative hypotheses. Surely one would like to say, for example, '287 sentences will set this parameter correctly', but our understanding of language acquisition at this point is far too primitive to make statements with that level of accuracy.

But there is another, equally suggestive, way of evaluating Pullum's claim: we situate the case of structure dependency in a *comparative* setting of language acquisition. That is, we need an independent yardstick to quantitatively relate the amount of relevant linguistic experience to the outcome of language acquisition—the variational model offers just that.

First and foremost, we must take an independent case in acquisition, for which we have good knowledge of children's developmental time course, and for which we can also obtain a corpus frequency of the relevant evidence. The null subject phenomenon is a perfect example.

As reviewed earlier, English children's subject use reaches adult level at around 3;0 (Valian 1991). This is comparable to the age of the children whose knowledge of structure dependence was tested by Crain & Nakayama (1987): the youngest group was at 3;2. In both cases, the learners make a binary choice: Valian's children have to determine whether the language uses overt subjects, and Crain & Nakayama's children would, if Pullum were correct, have to rule out the possibility that language is structure-dependent but not linear. Under the present model—in fact, under any quantitative model of language acquisition—comparability in the completion of two acquisitions must entail comparability in the frequency of their respective evidence.[8] If English subject use is gradually learned on the basis of *there* expletive sentences, which represent roughly 1.2% of all sentences, then one would expect sentences like (64) and (65), which supposedly establish structure dependence, also to be close to 1.2% in the input data.

Which takes us to a second problem in Pullum's argument: we must start with *realistic* corpora of children's linguistic input. The *Wall Street Journal* hardly fits the bill, a point that Pullum himself

---

[8] One may reject models that do *not* predict such frequency–development correlations, on the ground that the comparable time courses of subject acquisition and V2 acquisition (section 4.1.2) would be an accident.

acknowledges. Realistic counts can be obtained from CHILDES. For example, based on fifty-six files in the Nina corpus, we found:

(67) 46,499 sentences, of which 20,651 are questions, of which
   a. None were *yes/no* questions of the type in (64).
   b. Fourteen were *Wh* questions of the type in (65), exhaustively listed below:
      i. Where's the little red duck that Nonna sent you? (NINA02.CHA)
      ii. Where are the kitty cats that Frank sent you? (NINA03.CHA)
      iii. What is the animal that says cockadoodledoo? (NINA04.CHA)
      iv. Where's the little blue crib that was in the house before? (NINA05.CHA)
      v. Where's the other dolly that was in here? (NINA05.CHA)
      vi. What's this one up here that's jumping? (NINA05.CHA)
      vii. Where's the other doll that goes in there? (NINA05.CHA)
      viii. What's the name of the man you were yesterday with? (NINA10.CHA)
      ix. What color was the other little kitty cat that came to visit? (NINA28.CHA)
      x. Where's the big card that Nonna brought you? (NINA38.CHA)
      xi. And what was the little girl that came who also had whiskers? (NINA41.CHA)
      xii. Where's the card that Maggie gave you for Halloween? (NINA41.CHA)
      xiii. Nina # where are the pants that daddy sent you? (NINA43.CHA)
      xiv. Where are the toys that Mrs Wood told you you could bring home? (NINA46.CHA)

This puts the frequency of relevant evidence at approximately 0.03%:[9] that is forty times lower than 1.2%, the amount of

---

[9] Following Sampson (1989), Pullum argues that sentences like (i) also disambiguate the correct rule from the first auxiliary hypothesis:

(i) If you don't need this, can I have it?

If the underlying representation of (i) is [*If you don't need this, I can have it*], the first auxiliary rule would front either *don't* or *can*, producing erroneous output. However, this line of reasoning would not work if children know where sentence boundaries are, evidence needed to settle on one of two binary choices by around the third birthday.

Just to confirm that the Nina statistics are no accident, we considered another corpus, that of Adam. In an earlier paper, Legate (1999) finds the following:

(68) In a total of 20,372 sentences, 8,889 were questions, of which
    a. None were *yes/no* questions of the type in (64).
    b. Four were *Wh* questions of the type in (65):[10]
        i. Where's the part that goes in between? (ADAM43.CH)
        ii. What is the music it's playing? (ADAM37.CHA)
        iii. What's that you're drawing? (ADAM47.CHA)
        iv. What was that game you were playing that I heard downstairs? (ADAM52.CHA)

which gives a frequency of 0.01%.

Furthermore, crucial evidence at a frequency around 0.01% may not be frequent enough to be distinguishable from noise. Interestingly, the canonical type of critical evidence, [aux [NP aux]], appeared not even once in all 66,971 adult sentences. Hence the original APS not only stands unchallenged, but is in fact strengthened: the knowledge of structure dependence in syntax, as far as we can test quantitatively and comparatively, is available to children in the absence of experience.[11] And the conclusion

---

i.e. that the punctuation between two clauses signals a fresh start. There is, however, evidence that children do recognize sentence boundaries, for which perhaps even low-level acoustic cues suffice (Fisher & Tokura 1996). In any case, we only found 10 such sentences in the Nina corpus, 4 of which contain the special symbol #, which encodes a significant pause separating two clauses. Even including these examples would still give a frequency far lower than 1.2%.

[10] Of these, it is not even clear whether the equative sentences (68b-iii) and (68b-iv) necessarily count as evidence against the first auxiliary hypothesis. The child might analyze them with the *wh* word in the subject position and the complex NP in the object position (although this is arguably not the analysis ascribed to these questions in adult grammar). The Nina sentences in (67b-iii), (67b-vi), and (67b-viii) are of this type as well. There is an additional *wh* question containing a complex NP in the Adam files, however the context reveals that it is unambiguously an echo question with the *wh* word in subject position: Adam: *Dat's de funniest bird I ever saw.* Mother: *What is the funniest bird you ever saw?*

[11] In any case, the claim that children entertain the first auxiliary hypothesis for question formation is false. There is, of course, no way to prove that no possible

then is Chomsky's (1975: 33): 'the child's mind ... contains the instruction: Construct a structure-dependent rule, ignoring all structure-independent rules. The principle of structure-dependence is not learned, but forms part of the conditions for language learning.'

## 4.3 The nature of null subjects in children

We now turn to a detailed analysis of null subjects (NS) in English children in comparison to Chinese and Italian children. We begin with a typology of subject use across languages, which serves to establish the nature of the candidate grammars that compete during acquisition.

To recover the referential content of a null subject, optional subject grammars employ one of two (almost inevitable) strategies (Huang 1984). In one group that includes languages like Italian and Spanish, a null subject is identified via unambiguous agreement (number, person, gender) morphology on the verb. It seems that unambiguous morphological agreement is only a necessary condition for the Italian type pro-drop. That is, there is no reason that unambiguous agreement would *force* a language to be pro-drop. There are Scandinavian languages such as Icelandic with full agreement paradigms but no (systematic) pro-drop. That is,

(69) a. Pro-drop ⇒ unambiguous agreement.
b. Unambiguous agreement does not imply pro-drop.

In the group of languages that includes Chinese, a null subject is identified via linking to a discourse topic, which serves as its antecedent. Because of the differences in the identification mechanism, Chinese and Italian show different distributions of null arguments.

---

structure-independent hypothesis is *ever* entertained; no such proof can exist, given the normal ethics of human subject experimentation. However, whatever alternative hypothesis one conjures up, one had better crank out some frequency counts not far from 1.2% for relatively late 'learnings'.

First, Italian does not allow arbitrary null objects (NO) (Rizzi 1986). In contrast, Chinese does freely allow NO (Huang 1984), which, like null subjects, can be recovered by linking the empty pronominal to a discourse topic:

(70) TOPIC$_1$ [Zhangsan kanjian-le $e_1$].   ($e_1$ = him)
 TOPIC$_1$ [Zhangsan saw-ASP him$_1$].
 'Zhangsan saw him.'

However, Chinese NS is more restrictive than Italian. When a topic phrase (Top) is fronted, subject drop in Chinese is grammatical only if Top is not a possible antecedent for the null subject, for otherwise the linking to discourse topic is disrupted. More specifically, Chinese NS is possible (71a) when Top is an adjunct, which can never be the antecedent of a dropped subject, and not possible (71b) when Top is an argument (object).

(71) a. Zai gongyuan-li$_2$, [$e_1$ $t_2$ da-le ren].   ($e_1$ = John)
  In park-LOC, [$e_1$ $t_2$ beat-ASP people].
  'It is in the park [but not at school] that John beat people up.'
 b. *Sue$_2$, [$e_1$ xihuan $t_2$]. ($e_1$ = John)
  Sue$_2$, [$e_1$ likes $t_2$].
  'It is Sue [but not Mary] that John likes.'

Italian identifies null subjects through agreement morphology, and does not have the restrictions on subject drop seen above in Chinese. Subjects can be dropped freely in nominal and non-nominal Wh questions,[12] as shown below:

(72) a. Chi$_2$ $e_1$ ha baciato $t_2$?
  Who$_2$ has(3SGM) kissed $t_2$?
  'Who has he kissed?'
 b. Chi$_3$ $e_1$ credi che $e_2$ ami $t_3$?
  Who$_3$ $e_1$ think(2SG) that $e_2$ loves(3SGF) $t_3$?
  'Who do you think she loves?'

---

[12] Following Chomsky (1977) and many others, we adopt the generalization that topicalization and Wh movement are essentially the same process (movement to [Spec,CP]), for they share many syntactic and semantic properties. Since Chinese cannot front Wh phrases (in questions or any other constructions), only topicalization data can be given in (71).

c. Dove$_2$  hai         $e_1$ visto Maria $t_2$?
   Where$_2$ have(2SG) $e_1$ seen Maria $t_2$?
   'Where have you seen Maria?'

The differences between Chinese, English, Italian subject use are summarized below:

(73) a. The Chinese type: object drop, no subject drop with argument topicalization.
   b. The English: no object drop, obligatory subject, use of expletive *there*.
   c. The Italian: no object drop, unrestricted subject drop, rich Agreement morphology.

We shall see how such differences play out their roles in child language acquisition, disambiguating these grammars from one another. In addition, we shall see how these differences are repeated in (English) children's acquisition of subject use. We will again stress that the learner does not actively search for the patterns in (72) to identify their target grammar, as in a cue-based learning model. Rather, the grammars are probabilistically selected to analyze incoming sentences, and they will face different outcomes in different linguistic environments. For example, both English and Italian grammars will be punished in a Chinese environment when a null object sentence is encountered. Only the target grammar wins out in the end.

### 4.3.1   The early acquisition of Chinese and Italian subject drop

Here we study the acquisition of subject use in Chinese and Italian children; we turn to English children in section 4.3.2. Throughout our discussion, when we refer to a particular language, we mean the property of subject use in that *type* of I-language grammar. So, when we say a 'Chinese grammar', we mean that the type of grammar that employs discourse-based argument drop.

Consider first how a Chinese child rules out English and Italian grammars. Here, null object sentences like (70) are unambiguous evidence for a Chinese-like grammar. A study by Wang et al. (1992) shows that Chinese adults use a fair amount of object drop sentences in speech to children (11.6%, computed from their appendix B) as well as among themselves (18%, computed from their appendix D). In section 4.1 we empirically established that 7% of unambiguous evidence suffices for very early acquisition, as in the mastery of finite verb raising by French children (Pierce 1989). We thus predict that from very early on, Chinese children have eliminated English and Italian grammars, and converged on the remaining grammar, the target.

This prediction seems correct. Wang et al. (1992: appendix C) find that the youngest group of Chinese children (2-year-olds) drop subjects 55.728% and objects 20.192%. The figures for subject drop is slightly higher than for adults, for whom the ratios are 45.852% and 18.000% (appendix D). This is probably due to the fact that the statistics from Wang et al. are based on elicitation, which clearly introduces more contextual situations for subject drop. Our own study of production data yields the figure of 49%.[13]

Additional evidence for early mastery by Chinese-speaking children of the target form of subject drop comes from an elicitation experiment carried out by Wang et al. in the same study (1992: 240–2). They tried to get Chinese children to use expletives, the equivalent of the weather *it* in English, as in (74):[14]

(74) a. [e] Xiàyǔ-le
       (It) rain-ASP.
       '[It] is raining.'
   b. [e] Kànshàngqù [e] yào    xiàyǔ-le.
      [It] seems      (it) going to  rain-ASP.
      '[It] seems that (it) is going to rain.'

In general, Chinese children in all age groups leave the subject position null.

---

[13] We used a random sample of 100 sentences each from 3 children: All are from the Beijing corpus in CHILDES. All sentences contained a verb or a predicate, and thus an opportunity for subject drop.
[14] Chinese adults may use 'Tiān' (sky) in place of *it* in English, but this is purely stylistic.

Let us now turn to Italian children. Recall that Chinese does not allow subject drop when an argument assumes the topic position (71b), and Italian does (with a fronted argument *Wh* phrase). This means that every subjectless question with an argument (object) *Wh* question punishes a Chinese grammar, and of course an English grammar as well.

It is known that approximately 70% of adult utterances have dropped subjects (Bates 1976, cited in Caselli et al. 1995). We also know that *Wh* questions are one of the most frequent constructions children are exposed to. We estimate that about 10% of all sentences are object questions involving empty subjects: again, the lower bound of 7% then warrants an early acquisition. This prediction is confirmed by Valian's findings (1991): at both of the developmental stages investigated (1;6–1;10 and 2;0–2;5), Italian children drop subjects in about 70% of sentences, roughly the same as the figures in adult speech reported in the references cited above.

## 4.3.2 English children speak Chinese

Finally, we consider how English children come to learn that their language uses an obligatory subject grammar, ruling out the Chinese and Italian grammars that are also made available by UG.

We first claim that the Italian grammar can very rapidly be eliminated by English children on the basis of their knowledge of agreement morphology. In Chapter 3 we reviewed the very strong evidence that young children's agreement morphology is near-perfect. Phillips (1995: 327), reviewing a number of crosslinguistic studies, observes that 'in languages with overt agreement morphology, children almost always use the agreement morphemes appropriate to the argument being agreed with'. Again, Guasti (1992) found that three young Italian children used agreement morphology correctly in more than 95% of all contexts; see e.g. Clahsen & Penke (1992) for similar findings in German, Torrens (1995) for Catalan, Levy & Vainikka (1999) for Hebrew.

Children's near-perfect knowledge of agreement morphology plays an important role in grammar competition. It rules out the Italian grammar that is almost extensionally a superset of English—minus the presence of *there*-type expletives. Hence, one must understand the variational model and the evaluation of grammar–sentence compatibility in the sense of strong generative capacity (cf. section 2.2.2). We remarked earlier in (69) that unambiguous agreement is a necessary condition for pro-drop. Thus, if a language does not have unambiguous agreement, then it cannot be pro-drop. Specifically, if an Italian grammar is chosen to analyze English input, the lack of unambiguous agreement in English causes the Italian grammar to fail and be punished as a result.[15]

The Chinese grammar is more difficult to rule out. Chinese employs discourse linking as the mechanism for null subject identification; morphology provides no useful information. The only evidence against the Chinese grammar is expletive *there* sentences, which constitute only 1.2% of all input sentences. Hence, with respect to subject use, we predict that English children ought to use an English grammar in coexistence with a Chinese grammar for an extended period of time.

The claim of grammar coexistence attributes English child NS to the presence of the Chinese grammar, which is probabilistically accessed. This directly explains the fact that 2-year-old English children use a non-trivial amount of NS, but at a lower rate (30%) than Chinese children of the same age group (46.5%) (Wang et al.

---

[15] The acquisition of a language—Icelandic, say—with unambiguous agreement but not pro-drop raises some interesting questions. Note that an Italian-type grammar selected by an Icelandic learner will not be contradicted by agreement reasons. A possible reason for rejecting the pro-drop grammar may be some version of the Avoid Pronoun Principle (Chomsky 1981). It is well known that in pro-drop languages such as Italian and Spanish, the use of overt pronouns is unnatural for normal discourse, and is reserved only for focus, contrast, stress, etc. If so, then the presence of overt pronoun, despite (redundant) unambiguous agreement, may count against the pro-drop grammar—which, if true, again suggests that grammar-input analysis is not simply string compatibility, but turns on UG principles.

I would like to thank Norbert Hornstein for bringing this problem to my attention.

1992). We also predict that child English ought to contain a certain amount of null objects (NO), grammatically acceptable in Chinese. Such an account of NO does not appeal to performance factors (e.g. Bloom 1990, Valian 1991) that are usually hard to quantify. Furthermore, the presence of the Chinese grammar entails that the distributional patterns of English child NS ought to show characteristics of a Chinese grammar. To demonstrate this, we look at two quantitative predictions that are borne out below.

First, recall that in a Chinese-type grammar, NS is only possible in adjunct topicalizations (71a), but not in argument topicalizations (71b). Since we attribute English child NS to a Chinese grammar, we expect that NS will be possible in adjunct questions but not possible in argument (object) questions.[16] This prediction is strongly confirmed. During the NS stage of Adam (CHILDES: files 1–20), we found an almost categorical asymmetry of NS in adjunct and argument questions:

(75) a. 95% (114/120) of *Wh* questions with NS are adjunct (*how, where*) questions.
 b. 97.2% (209/215) of object questions (*who, what*) contain subjects.

The second prediction concerns the relative frequencies of NS and NO. Since both NS and NO are attributed to the Chinese grammar, we predict that the relative ratio of NS/OS will hold fairly constant across English and Chinese children in a same age group. This prediction is made as follows. Suppose that for Chinese children, NS ratio is $s$ and NO ratio is $o$, and that for English children, NS ratio is $s'$ and NO ratio is $o'$. Suppose further that, during the NS stage, English children access the Chinese grammar with the probability $p$, which leads to the NS and OS patterns in production.[17] Recall that Chinese children learn their grammar very early,

---

[16] The fronting of the *Wh* word in question formation, of course, is an early acquisition, as noted in section 3.1. Again, the parameter for *Wh* fronting and the subject parameter are set independently.

[17] Note that $p$ is a variable that diminishes over time when the Chinese grammar is on its way out.

showing adult-like performance; they hence use the Chinese grammar 100% of the time. Now if we scale up $p$ to 100%, that is, English children were to use the Chinese grammar *monolingually*, we expect their NS and OS ratios to be identical to those for Chinese children.[18] That is, $s' = sp$ and $o' = op$, which implies $s'/o' = s/o$.

The confirmation for this prediction is shown in Fig. 4.1, based on the statistics reported in Wang et al. (1992).[19] It plots the slopes of NO/NS for both Chinese and American children, which are virtually indistinguishable: the raw statistics are 20.192/55.728 = 36.2% and 8.308/25.885=32.1%, respectively.

Finally, we may add that the expletive subject elicitation study of Wang et al. (1992: 242) did succeed on American children, who alternately use null subjects (76) (as well as overt ones (77):

(76) a. It is raining. (SR: 2;8)
     b. It's rain. Rain. They can't come out. (DS: 2;10)

(77) a. No snow. (SR: 2;8)
     b. Snow. Raining. (DS: 2;10)

This again demonstrates the coexistence of both types of grammars.

The quantitative predictions reported here, including the categorical asymmetry in argument and adjunct questions and the relative ratio of NS/NO, is expected under the variational model of grammar competition. The model explicitly appeals to the syntactic properties of competing UG grammars given by theories of adult linguistic competence. Again, they cannot be made under performance-based theories that assume English children have an adult-like obligatory subject grammar and that null

---

[18] Assuming, without evidence to the contrary, that English and Chinese children are equally likely to encounter discourse situations in which NS and OS would be employed. Hence it is important to use statistics from a single study: the experimental design and counting procedure would be consistent for both American and Chinese children.

[19] We have used the statistics for American children between 2;0 and 3;0, when they are in the subject stage.

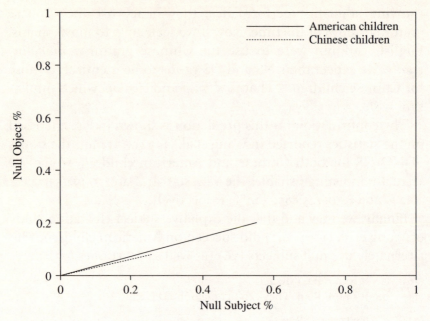

FIGURE 4.1. Chinese and English child NO/NS ratios

subjects result from performance factors that perturb the use of their grammar.[20] In addition, performance-based theories seem to be self-contradictory. If performance limitations are the cause of English child NS, why do not the same limitations affect Italian and Chinese children, resulting in NS (and NO) ratios higher than Italian and Chinese adults? In fact, it seems that Italian and Chinese children have adult-level subject usages from early on, as reviewed in section 4.3.1.

The recent optional infinitive (OI) based approach to null subject (e.g. Rizzi 1994, Sano & Hyams 1994, Hyams 1996, Wexler 1998), which holds that null subjects are licensed by non-finite root verbs, also says nothing about the quantitative findings reported. Furthermore, if the OI approach to NS were correct, it would predict that the OI stage and the NS stage should end at

---

[20] There is by now a large body of literature against the performance-based approach to NS; see e.g. Hyams & Wexler (1993), Roeper & Rohrbacher (1994), Bromberg & Wexler (1995), Waller (1997) and the present study.

roughly the same time. There is, however, prima facie evidence to the contrary.[21] For example, the OI stage for a Dutch child Hein (Haegeman 1995: table 4) essentially ended at 3;0 and 3;1, when his OI usage dropped to 4% and 6%. However, at 3;0 and 3;1 there were still 30% and 31% of NS sentences.

## 4.4 Summary

We summarize the key features and results of the variational model as applied to syntactic acquisition:

(78) a. Language acquisition can be modeled as a selectionist process in which variant grammars compete to match linguistic evidence.
b. Under the condition of explanatory continuity, the irregularity in child language and the gradualness of language development can be attributed to a probabilistic combination of multiple grammars, rather than to imperfect exercise of a single grammar.
c. Formal sufficiency and development compatibility can be simultaneously met in the variational model, for which the course of acquisition is determined by the relative compatibilities of the grammars with input data; such compatibilities, expressed in penalty probabilities, are quantifiable and empirically testable.

The variational theory offers a new interpretation of child language. The first step is the observation of non-uniformity in children's language: the deviation from the adult grammar they are acquiring. Second, we try to identify the grammars, which are not what the learner is exposed to but nevertheless are options allowed by UG (and possibly realized in the world of existing languages), and which, *collectively* with the target grammar, give a complete coverage of children's language. Third, we associate each of the competing grammars with its corresponding disconfirming evidence in the linguistic environment, i.e. input patterns that they are incompatible with. It is clear that both steps two and three are guided by linguistic theories and typology. Finally, we

---

[21] See Phillips (1995) for additional discussion that the correlation between OI and NS is weak.

may use naturalistic adult-to-child linguistic databases to access the penalty probabilities of the competing grammars. Quantitative predictions are then possible. The idiosyncratic properties of coexisting competing grammars will be repeated in children's language, as demonstrated in this chapter: Dutch children use Hebrew grammar, English children use Chinese grammar, etc. In future work, this procedure will be systematically applied to a wider range of topics in children's syntax.

# 5

# The Dynamics of Language Change

> An observed linguistic change can have only one source—a change in the grammar that underlies the observed utterances.
> Noam Chomsky and Morris Halle, *The Sound Patterns of English* (1968), p. 249

Language is not a random object, but is governed by UG principles and constraints that are ultimately grounded in human biology.[1] If our (linguistic) ancestors had brains like ours, then UG, as we understand it through our languages, would have governed their languages as well. And if UG defines the intrinsic space of language variations—past, present, and future—then the historical process of language change cannot step out of these boundaries. Thus, UG must be placed at a central position in the explanation of language change.

Equally important to the study of language change is language acquisition, long recognized by linguists as the medium through which language change is transmitted over time (e.g. Paul 1890, Halle 1962, Chomsky & Halle 1968, Andersen 1973, Lightfoot 1979). Ultimately, language changes because learners acquire grammars that are different from that of their parents. In addition, as children become parents, their linguistic expressions constitute the acquisition evidence for the next generation. Following Battye & Roberts (1995) and others, this iterative

---

[1] I owe a special debt to Ian Roberts, Tony Kroch, and Ann Taylor for their scholarship on the history of French and English. The statistics used in this chapter, indispensable for the sort of modeling reported here, are taken from their works.

process can be stated in the familiar distinction between E- and I-languages (Chomsky 1986) (see Fig. 5.1).

There is another crucial factor in language change: the external linguistic evidence available to our ancestors when they were language learners themselves. It determined the languages they acquired, and the linguistic evidence they provided for later generations. The process in Fig. 5.1 extrapolated over time specifies the dynamics of a formal model of language change.

These considerations suggest that a model of language acquisition must be an integral part of a model of language change. When one gives descriptions of a certain historical change—for example, the change of a parameter from one value to another—one must give an account, from a language-learning perspective, of *how* that change took place. Hence, the empirical conditions imposed on an acquisition model, outlined in Chapter 1, must apply to a language change model with equal force. Of these, two aspects deserve particular attention.

First, the model must in principle be able to make *quantitative* predictions about the direction of language change at time $t + 1$ and beyond, when presented with the composition of linguistic data time $t$. For example, one would like to make claims that when such and such patterns are found in certain distributions, linguistic change is bound to occur.

Second, one must follow the condition of explanatory continuity in studying language change. It is common to find in the literature appeals to social, political, and cultural factors to explain language change. However, this approach is not complete unless one develops a formal, quantitative, developmentally compatible,

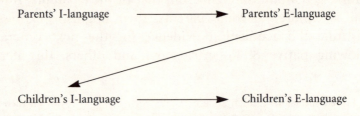

FIGURE 5.1. The dynamics of language acquisition and language change

and independently motivated model which details how such factors affect language acquisition. It is also common to find notions such as 'diachronic reanalysis', which claims that the learner under certain conditions will opt for a radical change in his grammar. Again, these claims can be substantiated only when supporting evidence is found in synchronic child language development.

This chapter extends the acquisition model to a study of language change that satisfies these requirements. It characterizes the dynamic interaction between the internal Universal Grammar and the external linguistic evidence, as mediated by language acquisition. We will again borrow insights from the study of biological evolution, where internal and external forces—genetic endowment and environmental conditions—interact in a similar fashion. Section 5.1 spells out the model and derives a number of formal properties, including a sufficient and necessary condition under which one grammar replaces another. In sections 5.2 and 5.3 we apply the model to explain the loss of V2 in Old French and the erosion of V2 in Old English.

## 5.1 Grammar competition and language change

### 5.1.1 *The role of linguistic evidence*

Given the dynamics of language change in Fig. 5.1, the fundamental question in language change is to identify the causal forces that result in generation $n + 1$ learning a language different from generation $n$.

Under the (innocent) assumption that UG and the algorithm of language acquisition, both biologically specified, did not change over the history of humans, the only source for the discrepancy between two generations of speakers must lie in the linguistic evidence: generation $n$ and $n + 1$ are exposed to sufficiently different linguistic evidence and thus form a different knowledge of language as a result.

This conclusion is warranted only when another logical

possibility is rejected. We must show that within a generation of speakers viewed as a population of individuals, it is not possible that, in spite of comparable linguistic evidence, *some* members of generation $n + 1$ should attain a different grammar from generation $n$, as a result of 'mis-learning'. We have three arguments against this possibility.

First, acquisition research shows that children are highly competent and robust learners: it seems improbable that, given sufficiently similar experience, children will attain languages that are substantially different (e.g. that a major syntactic parameter is set to a wrong value in a significant proportion of the population). Stylistics aside, all of us with similar experience attain core grammars that are very similar to each other.

Second, it has been observed that language change occurs on the scale of the entire population, not in scattered individual members, as Bloomfield (1927, cited in Hockett 1968: 12–13) comments:

It may be argued that change in language is due ultimately to the deviations of individuals from the rigid system. But it appears that even here individual variations are ineffective; whole groups of speakers must, for some reason unknown to us, coincide in a deviation, if it is to result in a linguistic change. Change in language does not reflect individual variability, but seems to be a massive, uniform, and gradual alteration, at every moment of which the system is just as rigid as at every other moment.

And finally, while one might attempt to invoke the idea of individual mislearning to explain historical change in *some* languages,[2] it leaves mysterious the relative stability in other

---

[2] Indeed, this is the approach taken by Niyogi & Berwick (1995), whose model of language change relies on misconvergence by triggering learners in the sense of Gibson & Wexler (1994). For them, some speakers converge to one grammar, while others to another; it is the proportion of these two kinds of speaker that changes. A main problem with this model, carried over from the triggering approach, is that it associates the learner with a unique grammar. This position is difficult to mention both developmentally (see the preceding chapters) and diachronically (Kroch 2001; more later). Another problem is that, according to simulations conducted on this model, the phenomenon of V2 cannot be lost, while actual languages such as English and French did lose V2.

languages, say, the rigidity of word order in Western Germanic languages.

We therefore reject mislearning (under sufficiently similar linguistic evidence) as a possible mechanism of language change. A question immediately arises: what makes the linguistic evidence for generation $n + 1$ different from that of the previous generation? There are many possibilities. For example, migration of foreign speakers might introduce novel expressions; social and cultural factors might also influence the distributional patterns of linguistic expressions used in a population. These are interesting and important topics of research, but are not relevant for a formal model of language change. This situation has a perfect parallel in the mathematical theory of natural selection, which concerns the predictable changes in the population once some new genotypes are introduced. The precise manner in which new genes arise, which could be mutation, migration, etc., is a separate question, which is often affected by too many contingencies to command a firm answer. After all, the world would have looked very different if the comet that led to the demise of dinosaurs had been off target. Similarly, the factors that alter the composition of linguistic evidence from generation to generation may also be generally unpredictable: the linguistic landscape, and indeed the world, might have looked very different had Napoleon's winter in Russia been a lot warmer.

Hence, we are chiefly concerned with the predictable consequences of such changes: what happens to language learners *after* the linguistic evidence is altered, and how does it affect the composition of the linguistic population as a result?

## 5.1.2 *A variational model of language change*

Suppose that, as a result of migration, genuine innovation, and other sociological and historical factors, a linguistic environment is established for a generation of language learners that is substantially different from that for the previous generation.

The expressions used in such an environment—call it $E_{G_1, G_2}$—can formally be viewed as a mixture of expressions generated by two independent sources: the two grammars $G_1$ and $G_2$. Further, suppose that a proportion $\alpha$ of $G_1$ expressions are incompatible with $G_2$, and a proportion $\beta$ of $G_2$ expressions are incompatible with $G_1$. Call $\alpha$ ($\beta$) the *advantage* of $G_1$ ($G_2$). Fig. 5.2 illustrates.

The variational approach views language acquisition as competition and selection among grammars. Recall from Chapter 2 that the fitness of individual grammars is defined in terms of their penalty probabilities:

(79) The penalty probability of a grammar $G_i$ in a linguistic environment $E$ is
$$c_i = \Pr(G_i \not\to s \mid s \in E)$$

The penalty probabilities ultimately determine the outcome of language acquisition:

(80) $\lim_{t \to \infty} p_1(t) = \dfrac{c_2}{c_1 + c_2}$

$\lim_{t \to \infty} p_2(t) = \dfrac{c_1}{c_1 + c_2}$

Suppose that at generation $n$, the linguistic environment $E_{G_1, G_2} = pG_1 + qG_2$, where $p + q = 1$. That is, in $E_{G_1, G_2}$, a proportion $p$ of expressions are generated by $G_1$, and a proportion $q$ of expressions are generated by $G_2$, and they collectively constitute the linguistic evidence to the learners in generation $n + 1$. The penalty probabilities of $G_1$ and $G_2$, $c_1$ and $c_2$, are thus $\beta q$ and $\alpha p$. The

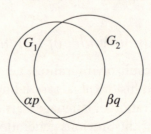

FIGURE 5.2. Two mutually incompatible grammars constitute a heterogeneous linguistic environment

results in (80) allow us to compute $p'$ and $q'$, the weights of $G_1$ and $G_2$ respectively, that are internalized in the learners of generation $n + 1$:

(81) The dynamics of a two grammar system:

$$p' = \frac{\alpha p}{\alpha p + \beta p}$$

$$q' = \frac{\beta q}{\alpha p + \beta q}$$

(81) shows that an individual learner in generation $n + 1$ may form a combination of two grammars $G_1$ and $G_2$ at a different set of weights from the parental generation $n$. Based on (81), we have:

(82) $\dfrac{p'}{q'} = \dfrac{\alpha p/(\alpha p + \beta q)}{\beta q/(\alpha p + \beta q)}$

$= \dfrac{\alpha p}{\beta q}$

In order for $G_2$ to overtake $G_1$, the weight of $G_2$ ($q$) internalized in speakers must increase in successive generations and eventually drive the weight of $G_1$ ($p$) to 0. That is, for each generation, it must be the case that $q' > q$, which is equivalent to $p'/q' < p/q$. Thus, we obtain a sufficient and necessary condition for grammar competition in a linguistic population:

(83) The fundamental theorem of language change
$G_2$ overtakes $G_1$ if $\beta > \alpha$: the advantage of $G_2$ is greater than that of $G_1$.

Recall that $\alpha$ and $\beta$ are presumably constants, which characterize the distributional patterns in the use of the respective languages. Note that we may not be able to estimate $\alpha$ and $\beta$ directly from historical context. The amount of sentences that contradict $G_1$ and $G_2$ are penalty probabilities of the competing grammars, i.e. $\alpha p$ and $\beta p$. However, (83) says that *if $q' > q$* ($G_2$ is on the rise), it must be the case that $\beta > \alpha$, *and*, if $\beta > \alpha$, $G_2$ will necessarily replace $G_1$. Hence, we have the following corollary:

(84) Once a grammar is on the rise, it is unstoppable.

Obviously, (83) and (84) are very strong claims, and should be closely scrutinized in future research.

Plotting the $q(t)$, the weight of $G_2$, as a function of time $t$, we obtain the familiar S-shape curve (Fig. 5.3) that has frequently been observed in language change (Weinreich et al. 1968, Bailey 1973, Kroch 1989, among many others), as the 'new' linguistic form gradually replaces the 'old' form.

The present model shares an important feature with the work of Clark & Roberts (1993), which extends the use of Genetic Algorithms in acquisition (Clark 1992). In both models, the outcome of language acquisition is determined by the compatibilities of grammars with linguistic evidence, in a Darwinian selectionist manner. However, they identify the final state of acquisition with a single grammar (cf. Niyogi & Berwick 1995). Therefore, when the linguistic evidence does not unambiguously

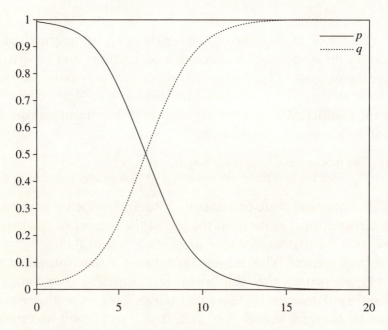

FIGURE 5.3. One grammar ($q$) replacing another ($p$) over time

identify a single grammar, as a realistic, inherently variable environment, they posit some general constraints on the learner, e.g. the elegance condition, which requires the learner to select the simplest among conflicting grammars. Aside from such explanatorily discontinuous assumptions that require independent justification, the hypothesis that a learner eventually selects a single grammar cannot be defended in face of the empirical evidence assembled by Kroch and his colleagues (e.g. Kroch 1989, Pintzuk 1991, Santorini 1992, Kroch & Taylor 1997, Kroch et al. 1997, Kroch 2001). They have shown that in historical texts during the period of language change, the grammatical competence of (mature) speakers must be attributed to multiple (I-language) grammars. For example, Santorini (1992) demonstrates that in early Yiddish subordinate clauses, individual speakers allowed both INFL-medial and INFL-final options. (85a) is an example of INFL-final, and (85b) is an example of INFL-medial. It is significant that both examples are from a single source (Prossnitz 1579; 2, 6):

(85) a. vas er zeyn tag fun zeynm r[ebe] gilernt *hat*
what he his day from his rabbi learned has
'what he learned from his rabbi in his day'
b. d[a]z der mensh *git* erst *oyf* in di hikh
that the human goes first up in the height
'the people first grow in height'

For the purpose of this study, we assume that all speakers in a linguistic community are exposed to identical linguistic experience, and that a speaker's linguistic knowledge is stable after the period of language acquisition. It is possible to incorporate these spatial and temporal variables into the model, which may be aided by the well-established models of population genetics and evolutionary ecology. We leave these options for further research.

To summarize the theoretical considerations in this section, we have extended the variational model of language acquisition to a population of learners and presented some analytic results concerning the dynamic system thus construed. We conclude that heterogeneity in the linguistic evidence, however introduced, is a prerequisite for language change. Once the homogeneity is punctured, language learners form internal representations of coexisting grammars. The propagation of such grammars in successive generations of individual learners defines the dynamics of language change. We now put the variational model of language change to the test.

## 5.2 The loss of V2 in French

Old French (OF) had a cluster of properties, including V2 and pro-drop, that are lost in Modern French (ModF). The following examples are taken from Clark & Roberts (1993):

(86) Loss of null subjects
    a. *Ainsi s'amusaient bien cette nuit. (ModF)
       thus [they] had fun that night.
    b. Si firent grant joie la nuit. (OF)
       thus [they] made great joy the night.

(87) Loss of V2
    a. *Puis entendirent-ils un coup de tonnerre. (ModF)
       then heard-they a clap of thunder.
    b. Lors oïrent ils venir un escoiz de tonoire. (OF)
       then heard they come a clap of thunder.

In this section, we will provide an analysis for the loss of V2 under the variational model. All examples and statistics cited in the remainder of this section are taken from Roberts (1993, henceforth R).

Recall that in order for a ModF SVO grammar to overtake a V2 grammar, it is required that the SVO grammar has a greater 'advantage'. That is, there must be more sentences in the linguistic evidence that are incompatible with the V2 grammar than with the SVO grammar. (88) shows the advantage patterns of V2 over SVO, and vice versa:[3]

---

[3] Again, for simplicity, we follow Lightfoot (1991) to consider only degree-0 sentences as linguistic input, although nothing hinges on this assumption.

(88) a. Advantage of V2 grammar over SVO grammar
V2 → s but SVO ↛ s: VS (XVSO, OVS)
b. Advantage of SVO grammar over V2 grammar:
SVO → s but V2 ↛ s: V > 2 (SXVO, XSVO)

If the distribution patterns in modern V2 languages are indicative of those of ancient times, we can see that the V2 constraint is in general very resilient to erosion. In languages like German, the V2 constraint is very strongly manifested. Matrix V > 2 patterns are restricted to a small number of adverbs and other specific lexical items, and are quite rare in distribution:

(89) Rare V > 2 patterns in modern German
... denn Johann hat gestern das Buch gelesen.
... so Johann had yesterday the book read.

Statistical analysis of Dutch, German, Norwegian, and Swedish (cited in Lightfoot 1997: 265) shows that about 70% of all sentences in V2 languages are SVO, and about 30% are VS patterns, which include XVSO and OVS. Our own counts, based on a Dutch sample of adult-to-child speech reported in section 4.1.2, are similar: 66.8% SVO, 23% XVSO, and 1.2% OVS. In contrast, based on the Penn Treebank (Marcus et al. 1993), a corpus of modern English, we found that only about 10% of all sentences have V > 2 word order:

(90) V > 2 patterns in modern English
a. He always reads newspapers in the morning.
b. Every evening Charles and Emma Darwin played backgammon.

Therefore, the 10% advantage of SVO grammar, expressed in V > 2 patterns, cannot throw off a V2 grammar, which has 30% of VS patterns to counter.

If the V2 constraint is so resilient, why did V2 succumb to SVO in French? The reason, in our view, is that OF was also a null subject language.

Recall that the advantage of V2 grammar over SVO grammar is expressed in VS patterns. However, this advantage would be considerably diminished if the subject were dropped to yield [X V pro] patterns: a null subject SVO grammar (like modern Italian) can analyze such patterns as [X (*pro*) V].(91) shows the prevalence of subject drop in early Middle French:

(91)
| Text | SV % | VS % | NullS % | |
|---|---|---|---|---|
| Froissart, *Chroniques* (c.1390) | 40 | 18 | 42 | |
| 15 Joyes (14esme Joye) (c.1400) | 52.5 | 5 | 42.5 | |
| Chartier, *Quadrilogue* (1422) | 51 | 7 | 42 | (R: 155) |

The 30% advantage in non-pro-drop V2 languages has been reduced to 5–18% in the pro-drop MidFr. As the same time, V > 2 patterns have gone from fairly sparse (about < 5%) in OF (R: 95) to 11–15% in early MidFr, as the class of sentence-initial XPs that do not trigger SV inversion was expanded (Vance 1989). (92) shows some representative examples:

(92) V > 2 patterns in early MidFr
    a. Lors la royne *fist* Santré appeler.
       then the queen made Santré to-call.
       'Then the queen had Saintré called.'
    b. Et a ce parolles le roy *demanda* quelz prieres
       And at these words the king asked what requests
       ilz faisonient
       they made.
    c. Apres disner le chevalier me *dist* . . .
       after dinner the knight to-me said . . .
       'After dinner the knight said to me . . .'

(93), which is based the same three texts in (91), shows the frequency of V > 2 patterns in MidFr:

(93)
| Text | V > 2 % | |
|---|---|---|
| Froissart, *Chroniques* (c.1390) | 12 | |
| 15 Joyes (14esme Joye) (c.1400) | 15 | |
| Chartier, *Quadrilogue* (1422) | 11 | (R: 148) |

Comparing (93) with (91), we see that at the early MidFr stage there were more V > 2 sentences than VS sentences, due to the effect of subject drop. Thus, following the corollary in (84), it must be the case that an SVO grammar (plus pro-drop) has an advantage over an OF V2 grammar (plus pro-drop). V2 in French was doomed, as predicted.

Our analysis of the loss of V2 in French crucially relies on the fact that null subject was lost after V2 was lost. R shows that this was indeed the case. In late fifteenth century and early sixteenth centuries, when SVO orders had already become 'favored', there was still significant use of null subjects, as the statistics in (94) demonstrate:

(94) The lasting effect of pro-drop in MidFr

|  | SV % | VS % | NullS % |  |
|---|---|---|---|---|
| Anon., *Cent Nouvelles Nouvelles* (1466) | 60.2 | 10 | 12 |  |
| Anon., *Le Roman de Jehan de Paris* (1495) | 60 | 10 | 30 |  |
| Vigneulles, CNN (1505–15) | 60 | 11 | 29 | (R: 155, 199) |

Overall, the mean figures for the relevant patterns are shown below:

(95)

|  | SV % | VS % | NullS % |  |
|---|---|---|---|---|
| 15th century | 48 | 10 | 42 |  |
| 16th century | 77 | 3 | 15 | (R: 199) |

The decline and eventual disappearance of VS patterns are the result of the SVO grammar winning over the V2 grammar. We see that in the sixteenth century, when V2 almost completely evaporated, there was still a considerable amount of subject drop. This diachronic pattern is consistent with our explanation for the loss of V2 in Old French.

We believe that the present analysis may be extended to other western European Romance languages, which, as is well known, all had V2 in medieval times. Under the present model of grammar competition, it is no accident that all such languages at one time had pro-drop, as in Old French, and many still do, as in Italian, Spanish, etc. It appears that the combination of pro-drop and V2 are intrinsically unstable, and will necessarily give away to an SVO (plus pro-drop) grammar. Without direct statistics from the history of these languages, we can extrapolate from their modern forms. It is reported (Bates 1976, cited in Caselli et al. 1995) that modern Italian uses pro-drop in 70% of all sentences; as a result, the 30% advantage of a V2 grammar over an SVO grammar (in VS sentences) would be reduced to 30% × 30% = 9%. Now this is a figure already lower than the approximately 10% of V > 2 sentences in which an SVO grammar has an advantage over a V2 grammar. This would necessarily lead to the demise of V2.

## 5.3 The erosion of V2 in Middle English

We now turn to the erosion of V2 in Middle English. Unless specified otherwise, all our examples and statistics are taken from Kroch & Taylor (1997, henceforth K&T). Our interpretation of the historical facts supports and formalizes their analysis.

### 5.3.1 Word order in Old English

K&T show that Old English (OE) is, generally speaking, a Germanic language similar to Yiddish and Icelandic. Its peculiarities lie in the distribution of its V2 patterns, which are different from modern West Germanic languages such as Dutch and German (van Kemenade 1987, Pintzuk 1991, K&T).

In OE, when the subject is an NP, the finite verb is in the second position:

(96) V2 with NP subjects in OE
    a. þæt hus    hæfdon Romane to   ðæm anum tacne
       that building had    Romans with the   one   feature
       geworht
       constructed
    b. þær wearþ se cyning Bagsecg ofslægen
       there was   the king   Bagsecq slain

In contrast, a pronominal subject precedes the verb, creating superficially V3 patterns with a non-subject topic phrase:

(97) V3 with pronoun subjects in OE
    a. Ælc yfel he mæg don.
       each evil he can   do.

    b.  scortlice ic hæbbe nu  gesæd ymb þa þrie dælas...
        briefly I have    now spoken about the three parts
    c.  Ōfter his gebede he ahof þæt cild up...
        after his prayer he lifted the child up

The subject pronoun is often analyzed as a clitic (van Kemenade 1987, Pintzuk 1991).

Furthermore, there are genuine V3 patterns when the topic position is occupied by a certain class of temporal adverbs and adjuncts. In these constructions, the subject, pronominal or phrasal, precedes the verb:

(98)  V3 with XP topics in OE
    a.  Her        Oswald se eadiga arcebisceop forlet  þis lif
        in-this-year Oswald the blessed archbishop forsook this life
    b.  On þisum geare Willelm cyng geaf Raulfe     eorle Willelmes
        In this    year William king gave [to] Ralph earl William's
        dohtor    Osbearnes sunu
        daughter Osborn's  son

The V2 constraint is uniformly obeyed in questions, where the verb raises to C and the subject, be it pronoun or NP, is in the postverbal position:

(99)  Verb raising to C in OE
    a.  hwi sceole we oþres    mannes niman?
        why should we another man's   take
    b.  þa    ge-mette he sceaðan
        then met      he robbers
    c.  ne mihton hi    nænigne fultum æt   him begitan
        not could   they not-any help    from him get
    d.  hæfdon hi   hiora onfangen ær     Hæsten to Beamfleote come
        had      they them received  before Hæsten to Benfleet    came

## 5.3.2 *The southern dialect*

K&T show that there was considerable dialectical variation with respect to the V2 constraint in the period of early Middle English (ME). Specifically, the southern dialect essentially preserved the V2 of Old English: preposed XPs, with exception of a certain class of adverbs and adjuncts noted earlier, generally trigger subject–verb inversion with full NP subjects but rarely with pronoun subjects (see Table 5.1).

Following van Kemenade (1987), we relate the eventual loss of V2 in English to the loss of subject cliticization. The loss of subject cliticization (and that of word-order freedom in general) can further be linked to impoverishment of the morphological case system of pronouns; see Kiparsky (1997) for a possible theoretical formulation of this traditional idea. Recall the V3 patterns in the southern dialect of early ME, which are manifested in sentences with pronominal subjects (98) and certain adverb and adjunct topics (98), schematically shown as in (100):

(100)   XP subject-pronoun $V_{FIN}$ ...

With the impoverishment and eventual loss of the morphological case system, clitics are no longer possible. Therefore, patterns such as (100) were no longer compatible with an OE type V2 grammar. However, they *were* compatible with an SVO grammar with the subject-pronoun treated as a DP, as in modern English. Examining Table 5.1, we see that 62% (511/825) of all matrix sentences are of the V > 2 pattern of the pattern (100) and 38% (314/825) are of the VS pattern. When subject pronouns could not be analyzed as clitics any more but only as NPs, the SVO grammar would have had an advantage over the V2 grammar, and eventually rose to dominance. The loss of the morphological case system makes the loss of V2 possible, and the

TABLE 5.1.   V2 in southern early Middle English

| Preposed XP | NP subjects % inverted | Pronoun subjects % inverted |
| --- | --- | --- |
| NP complements | 93  (50/54) | 5  (4/88) |
| PP complements | 75  (12/16) | 0  (0/11) |
| Adj. complements | 95  (20/21) | 33  (7/21) |
| þa/then | 95  (37/39) | 72  (26/36) |
| now | 92  (12/13) | 27  (8/30) |
| PP adjuncts | 75  (56/75) | 2  (2/101) |
| Adverbs | 57  (79/138) | 1  (1/182) |

Adapted from Kroch et al. (2000: table 1).

competition between the SVO grammar and the OE V2 grammar is straightforwardly captured in the present model of language change.

Notice that we immediately have an account for the so-called 'residual V2' in modern English questions, certain negations, etc. Recall that in (99), we saw that when V raises to C, both pronoun and NP subjects are in postverbal position. In other words, the linguistic evidence *for those constructions* has been homogeneous with respect to a V2 grammar throughout the history of English. Therefore, their V2 character is preserved.[4]

## 5.3.3 *The northern dialect and language contact*

In contrast to the southern dialect, K&T show that the northern dialect, under heavy Scandinavian influence, was very much like modern Germanic languages. The V2 constraint was uniformly and rigidly enforced, and one does not find the almost total asymmetry between pronoun and NP subjects in Old English and southern early Middle English.

As noted earlier, the V2 constraint exhibited in West Germanic languages is difficult to overthrow. This is due to the advantage a V2 grammar has over competing grammars such as SVO: V2 grammar generates VS sentences which punish SVO grammar, SVO grammar generates V > 2 sentences which punish V2 grammar, but VS sentences usually outnumber V > 2 sentences. In discussing the loss of V2 in Old French, we argued that subject drop in Old French considerably diminished V2's advantage, to a point where an SVO grammar, aided by an increase in V > 2 patterns, eventually won out. How did the northern early Middle English, a rigid V2 language without subject drop, evolve into an SVO language?

K&T show that the extensive contact between the northern and southern populations in the period of Middle English was essential

---

[4] More precisely, what has been preserved are the parametric choices that OE made in dimensions such as question and negation which the so-called 'residual V2' are attributed to.

to the eventual loss of V2 in English. They insightfully attribute the erosion of V2 to the competition of grammars in learners during language contact. This analysis is naturally formulated in the present model of language change. The northern V2 dialect, when mixed with the southern (essentially OE) language, constituted a heterogeneous linguistic environment for later generations of learners, who, instead of converging to a single grammar, attained a mixture of coexisting grammars. Table 5.2 shows the consequences of language contact in the northern dialect.

The effect of language contact is clear. Recall that prior to contact the northern dialect was much like Germanic languages, in which V2 is strongly enforced: Kroch et al. (2000) found subject–verb inversion in 93.3% of all sentences containing subjects. After contact (shown in Table 5.2), while NP subjects still in general follow subjects, the overall subject–verb inversion rate has dropped to 68.2% (208/305). This indicates that as a result of language contact and mixing, the V2 constraint in the northern dialect was considerably weakened. When the V2 constraint is sufficiently weakened, and if the morphological case system of the mixed language got lost, then an SVO grammar would have gradually taken over, in the manner described earlier for the loss of V2 in OE.

For the northern dialect, the initial contact with the southern dialect was crucial in the loss of V2.[5] That is, a West Germanic V2 language similar to the northern dialect would not lose V2 without language contact, even if its morphological case system was lost. Northern Germanic languages such as Swedish, Danish, and Norwegian, with an impoverished morphological case system but nevertheless strongly V2, presumably fall into this category. Once language contact was made, the homogeneity of linguistic evidence was broken, and two distinct grammars were formed by the learners. The loss of the morphological case system resulted in the loss of the clitics system, which further favored the SVO

---

[5] According to our theory, contact was not crucial for the Southern dialect to lose V2. The $V > 2$ patterns in the Southern dialect, which resulted from the lack of pronoun–verb inversion, might well have gradually eliminated V2 after the clitic system was lost.

TABLE 5.2. V2 (after languages contact) in the Northern MS (Thornton) of the Mirror of St Edmund

| Preposed XP | NP subjects % inverted | | Pronoun subjects % inverted | |
|---|---|---|---|---|
| NP complements | 100 | (8/8) | 64 | (16/25) |
| PP complements | 88 | (21/24) | 70 | (48/69) |
| Adj. complements | 100 | (10/10) | 25 | (2/8) |
| *then* | 86 | (6/7) | 51 | (24/47) |
| *now* | 100 | (4/4) | 82 | (14/17) |
| Adverbs | 80 | (20/25) | 57 | (35/61) |

*Source*: Kroch et al. (2000)

grammar and eventually drove it to complete dominance. K&T's thesis that language contact is the prerequisite for the loss of V2 in the northern dialect dovetails with our theoretical model rather nicely.

## 5.4 Limitations of the Model

The variational model of language change formalizes historical linguists' intuition of grammar competition, and directly relates the statistical properties of historical texts to the direction of language change. It is important to recognize that the competing forces—mutually incompatible grammars both of which are manifested in the input data—operate internally in the individual learner's mind/brain.

At the same time, we would like to stress the scope and limitation of this model. First, as is obvious, its applicability depends on the availability of historical data. Second, the model is constructed for syntactic change. Sound change, which is far more extensively researched, has different characteristics, although the structure of the model remains much the same: a 'UG' in the form of generative phonology, a concrete model of phonology learning, and a quantitative formulation of linguistic evidence. Principles of phonology and phonological learning are very likely to be different from those of syntax. Some preliminary work has been carried out in Yang (2002), on the basis of the Sussman–Yip algorithm (1996, 1997) and the phonological learning model developed in Chapter 3.

The most severe limitation is that the present model operates in a vacuum. First, it assumes that once a linguistic environment has been altered, populations of learners are left alone to evolve, devoid of further perturbation in linguistic evidence. Second, it does not consider sociological forces that may affect language learning, use, and ultimately, change (cf. Mufwene 2001). This is obviously an idealization that must be justified when applied to actual case studies. However, we believe that the virtue of this model lies in simplicity and predictiveness: the explanations for the loss of V2 in English and French, insofar as they are correct, did isolate a component of language change independent of the more intangible forces. We propose that this model be used as some sort of null hypothesis, again drawing a parallel with biology. Natural selection—the most deterministic force in evolutionary change as opposed to genetic drift, migration, neutral evolution etc.—is the null hypothesis, precisely because of its predictiveness. If the null hypothesis fails—*when* it fails is an empirical issue to be decided case by case—a more complicated or less predictive explanation may be invoked.

In any case, we hope that this work will contribute to a formal framework in which problems in language change can be studied with precision. Current work is extending the model to other cases in language change as well as the modeling of pidgin and croele phenomena.

# 6

# Summary

> A nativism of domain specific information needn't, of course, be *incompatible* with a nativism of domain specific acquisition mechanisms ... But I want to emphasize that, given his understanding of POSAs [Poverty of Stimulus Arguments], Chomsky can with perfect coherence claim that innate, domain specific PAs [Propositional Attitudes] mediate language acquisition, while remaining entirely agnostic about the domain specificity of language acquisition *mechanisms*.
> Jerry A. Fodor, 'Doing Without *What's Within*' (2001), pp. 107–8

To end this preliminary study of the variational approach to language, let us return to the abstract formulation of language acquisition to situate the variational model in a broader context of cognitive studies.

(101)  $\mathcal{L}: (S_o, E) \rightarrow S_T$

The variational model calls for a balanced view of $S_o$ and $\mathcal{L}$: domain-specific knowledge of language as innate UG as well as domain-neutral mechanism of learning. The connection between $S_o$ and $\mathcal{L}$ is made possible by the variational and probabilistic thinking central to Darwinian evolutionary theory. In variational thinking, children's deviation from adult language becomes the reflection of principled variations in human language; in probabilistic thinking, the continuous changes in the distributional patterns of child language are associated with discrete grammars of human language and their statistical distributions. The present approach, if correct, shows that a synthesis of Universal Grammar and learning is not only possible but desirable.

## 6.1 Knowledge and learning

We stress again that the admission of general learning/growth principles into language acquisition in no way diminishes the importance of UG in the understanding of natural language. UG allows the learner to go beyond unanalyzed distributional properties of the input data. Recall, as discussed in Chapter 4, the presence of Chinese-type topic drop during English children's Null Subject stage, as demonstrated by the almost categorical asymmetry in argument vs. adjunct NS questions (75) and the near-perfect match between Chinese and English children's NS/NO ratio (Fig. 4.1). It is inconceivable that such patterns can be explained without appealing to extremely domain-specific properties of grammars. The study of the variational model has been constantly guided by linguistic theories: for example, I would not have known where to look for coexisting grammars had it not been for the typology of three grammars (English, Chinese, and Italian) and their associated syntactic properties.

On the other hand, the variational model complements linguistic theories in two novel and interesting ways. First, the acquisition model leads one to find parallels between 'errors' in child language and adult languages elsewhere in the world, and to construct a unified solution to both problems. In Legate & Yang (2002), we pursue this line of thinking by exploiting the parallels between children's violation of the Binding Condition B and the apparent violation of the same condition in languages such as Old English. A unified account, which is ultimately a reformulation of Condition B, is provided there.

Second, the acquisition model provides an independent and theory-neutral tool for accessing the psychological status of linguistic theories.[1] A linguistic theory is an abstract description

---

[1] A similar and more familiar stance has been taken by J. D. Fodor and L. Frazier, among others, in the study of sentence processing as an evaluation criterion for linguistic theories.

of language that categorizes linguistic phenomena in insightful and interesting ways: parameters, for example, are one of the devices to capture important generalizations and natural classes. Just as there are infinitely many ways to slice up a cake, each a potential controversy at a party, disagreement arises when one linguist's insight is not shared by another.

If two competing linguistic theories, $T_1$ and $T_2$, are not merely restatements of each other—they often are—then they must capture different linguistic generalizations by making use of, say, two different parameters, $P_1$ and $P_2$. Suppose further that each gives a descriptively adequate account of some range of linguistic data. If these descriptions of linguistic competence are to have any direct bearing on features of linguistic performance such as acquisition,[2] the differences between $P_1$ and $P_2$ will be manifested in the acquisition of their respective parameter values in the target grammar: once we plug these two theories of $S_0$ into a theory-neutral model of learning $L$, the variational model, different developmental consequences ($D_1$ and $D_2$) will presumably result.

(102) $\quad T_1 \to \boxed{L} \to D_1$
$\quad\quad\quad T_2 \to \boxed{L} \to D_2$

(102) can be carried out straightforwardly: the identification of the relevant evidence to set target values, followed by the estimation of their frequencies in naturalistic corpora. Several aspects of $D_1$ and $D_2$ can then be evaluated in an acquisition context: regularities in overregularization errors (Chapter 3), developmental time course compared to empirically established baselines (sections 4.1 and 4.2), coexistence of competing parameter values (section 4.3), and, when available, diachronic trends through time (Chapter 5). All things being equal, theories more compatible with facts drawn from acquisition can be regarded as more plausible theories of Universal Grammar.

---

[2] A desirable feature of a competence theory but by no means a necessary one: see Yang (1996) for discussion in relation to the issue of 'psychological reality'.

One can immediately see that crude models of syntax, such as probabilistic context-free grammars (PCFG), which have recently attracted considerable attention in computational linguistics, psycholinguistics, and corpus-based studies, cannot be psychologically justified from an acquisition perspective. A PCFG, if a sufficiently large number of rules is allowed, can indeed approximate the distribution of sentences in all languages, and can be useful for many engineering applications.[3] Consider the fragment of a PCFG below:

(103) $S \xrightarrow{\alpha}$ Pronoun VP
$S \xrightarrow{\beta}$ pro VP, where $\alpha + \beta = 1$

(103) may be viewed as a model of the distribution of pronominal subjects across languages. For English, $\alpha$ would be 1, and in Italian, $\beta$ would be 1 (and thus $\alpha$, 0). Pitching (103) against English and Italian corpora may drive $\alpha$ and $\beta$ to the right values. The algorithm for updating these probabilities to fit the data may even be similar to that used in the variational model, and thus has the virtue of explaining the gradualness in child language.

However, the PCFG model can not be sustained from a developmental perspective. Consider another aspect of grammar, that of *Wh* movement, which roughly breaks into the overt *Wh* movement languages such as English and in-situ ones such as Chinese. A corresponding PCFG, which in principle can model the typology of *Wh* movement, may be:

(104) $S \xrightarrow{\gamma} Wh \ldots$
$S \xrightarrow{\delta} \ldots Wh$, where $\gamma + \delta = 1$.

As we know, *Wh* movement in English is acquired very early—virtually no *Wh* words are left behind (Stromswold 1990)—hence $\gamma$ must be driven to 1 very quickly. All this is done on what seems to be about a third of all English sentences that are *Wh* questions: this leaves the mystery of why the consistent use of English subjects, evidenced by almost all sentences, is learned so

---

[3] See Charniak (1996) for an overview, and some practical difficulties in PCFG learning.

late, i.e. why $\alpha$'s rise to 1 in (103) appears to be a much slower process.

Proponents of PCFG may protest that (103) and (104)—the most obvious kind—are not the type of rule they conjectured as psychological models. But my suspicion is that when the crosslinguistic facts of language acquisition and the nature of the input evidence are considered (e.g. section 4.3), the right model of PCFG (for pronominal subjects) may look like this:

(105) $S \xrightarrow{a} G_1$
$S \xrightarrow{b} G_2$
$S \xrightarrow{c} G_3$, where $a + b + c = 1$

with $G_1$, $G_2$, and $G_3$ being sophisticated hypotheses of languages, not unlike Chinese, English, and Italian-type grammars. That would be something we can all agree on.

The point of this discussion is that $L$, the mechanism for language acquisition, may indeed be a general process, and the study of $L$ may benefit from the study of learning from a number of disciplines. The hypothesis space of language, $S_0$, above all, must be studied with respect to adult language typologies and child language development, and all evidence points to a domain-specific body of knowledge. But these two aspects of learning may not be in conflict, as Jerry A. Fodor suggested in the quote at the beginning of this chapter.

Continuing this line of reasoning, we have already seen evidence that may resolve a number of contentious issues in linguistic theorizing. For example, subject uses in Italian, Chinese, and English children (section 4.3) suggest that the phenomenon of subject drop should be understood as a combination of the agreement-based type and the discourse identification type, as suggested by Huang (1984), and that the obligatory nature of overt subject is associated with the presence of pure expletives (e.g. *there*) in the language, as suggested by Hyams (1986) and Jaeggli & Safir (1989). Alternative formulation of subject use, which may be descriptively perfectly adequate, may lead to incorrect developmental predictions. Similarly, the demonstration that

English irregular verbs are organized in classes, defined by independent suffixation and readjustment rules, provides evidence for the traditional, rule-based conception of phonology.

## 6.2 Principles and variations

Variational thinking and statistical modeling proved instrumental in the theory of population genetics: they make a direct link between idealized and discrete Mendelian genetics and the variable patterns of biological evolution and diversity, which were apparently at odds. By the use of variational thinking and statistical modeling, the approach developed here may provide a principled way of bridging a similar gap, which lies between linguistic competence and linguistic performance, or between theoretical linguists' idealized and discrete grammars and the variabilities and gradients in language acquisition and use. As Richard Kayne (2000: 8) remarks, the subtle differences in speaker's grammatical intuitions lead one to conclude that there are as many 'grammars' as there are human speakers. While these differences may be attributed to different values of parameters, as Kayne suggests, it is also possible that speakers may acquired different parameter-value *weights* (section 2.4.4)— 'conflicting' parameter values may coexist—the result of very fine differences in learning and personal experience. Yet not all these differences in individual speakers are interesting to theoretical linguists, just as not all differences in individual organisms—we know that no two organisms are exactly the same—are interesting to theoretical biologists. Thus, the contribution of the variational model lies in the confirmation that theoretical inquiries along the lines of principles and parameters are perfectly compatible with variability studies, just as the search for deep genetic and developmental principles, which emphasize the commonalities among all or closely related organisms, are in no conflict with ecology or selective breeding, which emphasizes the differences.

Chomsky (1980) remarks that the learning of a language is much like the development and growth of physical organs. In an abstract sense, the variational model provides a possible realization of this suggestion. Competition and selection in the learning model immediately recall Hubel & Wiesel's (1962) classic study on the development of pattern-specific visual pathways. The selective growth of neural substrates has been proposed as a general model of learning and development (Changeux 1986, Edelman 1987). There seem to be neural groups, available at birth, that correspond to specific aspects (read: parameters) of stimulus—for example, orientations, shades, and colors of visual scenes. These groups develop in the manner of natural selection: only those that receive adequate stimulus specific to them survive and develop, and those that do not are weeded out.

Selectional growth at the behavioral level in other species has also been documented (Marler 1991).[4] Swamp sparrow song-learning goes through stages from plastic songs to stable songs, and the pattern is similar to child language. In the beginning there are many different forms of songs, characterized by a wide range of pitch, rhythm, and duration. Gradually the songs lose their variety until only one form is eventually retained, due to the discriminating effect of the songs in the environment. In the end, sparrows acquire their distinctive local 'dialects'.

While we have no precise theory as to how linguistic structures actually grow in the brain, the variational theory surely sounds like one, albeit at a very high level of idealization and abstraction. In a biologically continuous view, a human child in a specific linguistic environment, much like a swamp sparrow in New York or Minnesota, develops an ambient grammar out of many undifferentiated blueprints. The result is a largely stable language faculty.

I have aimed to show that the variational perspective resolves some puzzles in the UG approach to language acquisition, and

---

[4] I would like to thank Marc Hauser for emphasizing this relevance to me.

yields new insights on traditional problems as well as suggesting new problems. The investigations reported here are no doubt preliminary; I only hope that they have convinced the reader that this line of research is worth pursuing.

A long way to the vineyard after all.

# References

ALLEN, S. (1996). *Aspects of Argument Structure Acquisition in Inuktitut.* Amsterdam: John Benjamins.

ANDERSEN, H. (1973). Abductive and Deductive Change. *Language* 49: 765–93.

ANDERSON, S. R. (1992). *A-Morphous Morphology.* Cambridge: Cambridge University Press.

ATKINSON, R., BOWEVER, G., & CROTHERS, E. (1965). *An Introduction to Mathematical Learning Theory.* New York: Wiley.

BAILEY, C.-J. (1973). *Variation and Linguistic Theory.* Washington, DC: Center for Applied Linguistics.

BAKER, M. (1996). *The Polysynthesis Parameter.* Oxford: Oxford University Press.

—— (2001). *The Atoms of Language.* New York: Basic Books.

BARTO, A., & SUTTON, R. (1998). *Reinforcement Learning.* Cambridge, Mass.: MIT Press.

BATES, E. (1976). *Language and Context: The Acquisition of Pragmatics.* New York: Academic Press.

—— & ELMAN, J. (1996). Learning Rediscovered: A Perspective on Saffran, Aslin, and Newport. *Science* 274: 1849–50.

BATTYE, A., & ROBERTS, I. (1995). Introduction. In A. Battye & I. Roberts (eds.), *Clause Structure and Language Change.* Oxford: Oxford University Press, 1–30.

BEHRENS, H. (1993). Temporal Reference in German Child Language. Doctoral dissertation, University of Amsterdam.

BERKO, J. (1958). The Child's Learning of English Morphology. *Word* 14: 150–77.

BERTOLO, S., BROIHIER, K., GIBSON, E., & WEXLER, K. (1997). Characterizing Learnability Conditions for Cue-Based Learners in Parametric Language Systems. MS, Massachusetts Institute of Technology.

BERWICK, R. (1985). *The Acquisition of Syntactic Knowledge.* Cambridge, Mass.: MIT Press.

—— & NIYOGI, P. (1996). Learning from Triggers. *Linguistic Inquiry* 27: 605–22.

—— & WEINBERG, A. (1984). *The Grammatical Basis of Linguistic Performance.* Cambridge, Mass.: MIT Press.

BLOOM, L. (1970). *Language Development: Form and Function in Emerging Grammars.* Cambridge, Mass.: MIT Press.

BLOOM, P. (1990). Subjectless Sentences in Child Languages. *Linguistic Inquiry* 21: 491–504.

—— (1993). Grammatical Continuity in Language Development: The Case of Subjectless Sentences. *Linguistic Inquiry* 24: 721–34.

—— BARSS, A., NICOL, J., & CONWAY, L. (1994). Children's Knowledge of Binding and Coreference: Evidence from Spontaneous Speech. *Language* 70: 53–71.

BLOOMFIELD, L. (1927). Review of J. O. H. Jespersen, *The Philosophy of Grammar*. *Journal Of English and Germanic Philology* 26: 244–6.

BORER, H., & WEXLER, K. (1987). The Maturation of Syntax. In T. Roeper & E. Williams (eds.), *Parameter Setting*. Dordrecht: Reidel, 123–72.

BOSER, K. (1992). Early Knowledge of Verb Position in Children's Acquisition of German: An Argument for Continuity of Universal Grammar. Master's thesis, Cornell University.

DE BOYSSON-BARDIES, B. (1999). *How Language Comes to Children: From Birth to Two Years*. Cambridge, Mass.: MIT Press.

BROMBERG, H., & WEXLER, K. (1995). Null Subjects in Child Wh Questions. In C. Schütze, J. Ganger, & K. Broihier (eds.), *MIT Working Papers in Linguistics* 26: 221–47.

BROWN, R. (1973). *A First Language*. Cambridge, Mass.: Harvard University Press.

—— & HANLON, C. (1970). Derivational Complexity and order of Acquisition in Child Speech. In J. R. Hayes (ed.), *Cognition and the Development of Language*. New York: Wiley, 155–207.

BURZIO, L. (1991). The Morphological Basis of Anaphora. *Journal of Linguistics* 27: 81–105.

BUSH, R., & MOSTELLER, F. (1951). A Mathematical Model for Simple Learning. *Psychological Review* 68: 313–23.

—— & —— (1958). *Stochastic Models for Learning*. New York: Wiley.

BYBEE, J., & MODER, C. (1983). Morphological Classes as Natural Categories. *Language* 59: 251–70.

—— & SLOBIN, D. (1982). Rules and Schemas in the Development and Use of the English Past Tense. *Language* 58: 265–89.

CASELLI, M., BATES, E., CASADIO, P., FENSON, J., FENSON, L., SANDERL, L., & WEIR, J. (1995). A Cross-Linguistic Study of Early Lexical Development. *Cognitive Development* 10: 159–99.

CHANGEUX, J.-P. (1986). *The Neuronal Man*. Oxford: Oxford University Press.

CHARNIAK, E. (1996). *Statistical Natural Language Learning*. Cambridge, Mass.: MIT Press.

CHOMSKY, N. (1955/75). The Logical Structure of Linguistic Theory. MS, Harvard University and Massachusetts Institute of Technology. Published in 1975, New York: Plenum.

—— (1965). *Aspects of the Theory of Syntax*. Cambridge, Mass.: MIT Press.

—— (1975). *Reflections on Language*. New York: Pantheon.

—— (1977). On Wh-Movement. In P. Culicover, T. Wasow, & A. Akmajian (eds.), *Formal Syntax*. New York: Academic Press, 71–132.
—— (1980). *Rules and Representations*. New York: Columbia University Press.
—— (1981). *Lectures on Government and Binding*. Dordrecht: Foris.
—— (1986). *Knowledge of Language: Its Nature, Origin, and Use*. New York: Praeger.
—— (1995a). Language and Nature. *Mind* 104: 1–61.
—— (1995b). *The Minimalist Program*. Cambridge, Mass.: MIT Press.
—— (2000). Linguistics and Brain Sciences. In A. Marantz, Y. Miyashita, & W. O'Neil (eds.), *Image, Language, Brain*. Cambridge, Mass.: MIT Press, 13–28.
—— & Halle, M. (1968). *The Sound Patterns of English*. Cambridge, Mass.: MIT Press.
CHURCH, K. (1992). Comments on a Learning Model for a Parametric Theory in Phonology. In R. Levine (ed.), *Formal Grammar: Theory and Implementation*. Oxford: Oxford University Press, 318–26.
CLAHSEN, H. (1986). Verbal Inflections in German Child Language: Acquisition of Agreement Markings and the Functions They Encode. *Linguistics* 24: 79–121.
—— & PENKE, M. (1992). The Acquisition of Agreement Morphology and its Syntactic Consequences: New Evidence on German Child Language from the Simone Corpus. In J. Meisel (ed.), *The Acquisition of Verb Placement*. Dordrecht: Kluwer, 181–234.
—— & ROTHWEILER, M. (1993). Inflectional Rules in Children's Grammars: Evidence from the Development of Participles in German. *Yearbook of Morphology*, 1992: 1–34.
CLARK, E. (1993). *The Lexicon in Acquisition*. Cambridge: Cambridge University Press.
CLARK, R. (1992). The Selection of Syntactic Knowledge. *Language Acquisition* 2: 83–149.
—— & Roberts, I. (1993). A Computational Model of Language Learnability and Language Change. *Linguistic Inquiry* 24: 299–345.
COWIE, F. (1998). *What's Within: Nativism Reconsidered*. Oxford: Oxford University Press.
CRAIN, S. (1991). Language Acquisition in the Absence of Experience. *Behavioral and Brain Sciences* 14: 597–650.
—— & MCKEE, C. (1986). Acquisition of Structural Restrictions on Anaphora. *Proceedings of the North Eastern Linguistic Society* 16: 94–110.
—— & NAKAYAMA, M. (1987). Structure Dependency in Grammar Formation. *Language* 63: 522–43.
DEMUTH, K. (1989). Maturation and the Acquisition of Sesotho Passive. *Language* 65: 56–90.
DEPREZ, V., & PIERCE, A. (1993). Negation and Functional Projections in Early Grammar. *Linguistic Inquiry* 24: 25–67.

DRESHER, E. (1999). Charting the Learning Path: Cues to Parameter Setting. *Linguistic Inquiry* 30: 27–67.

—— & KAYE, J. (1990). A Computational Learning Model for Metrical Phonology. *Cognition* 34: 137–95.

EDELMAN, G. (1987). *Neural Darwinism: The Theory of Neuronal Group Selection*. New York: Basic Books.

ELMAN, J. (1990). Finding Structure in Time. *Cognitive Science* 14: 179–211.

—— (1991). Distributed Representations, Simple Recurrent Networks, and Grammatical Structure. *Machine Learning* 7: 195–224.

—— BATES, E., JOHN, M., KARMILOFF-SMITH, A., PARISI, D., & PLUNKETT, K. (1996). *Rethinking Innateness*. Cambridge, Mass.: MIT Press.

EMBICK, D., & MARANTZ, A. (in press). Cognitive Neuroscience and the English Past Tense: Comments on the Paper by Ullman et al. *Brain and Language*.

EMOND, J. (1978). The Verbal Complex V'–V in French. *Linguistic Inquiry* 9: 151–75.

FASSI-FEHRI, A. (1993). *Issues in the Structure of Arabic Clauses and Words*. Boston, Mass.: Kluwer.

FELIX, S. (1987). *Cognition and Language Growth*. Dordrecht: Foris.

FISHER, C., & TOKURA, H. (1996). Acoustic Cues to Grammatical Structure in Infant-Directed Speech: Cross-Linguistic Evidence. *Child Development* 67: 3192–218.

FODOR, J. A. (1998). *Concepts*. Oxford: Oxford University Press.

—— (2001). Doing Without *What's Within*: Fiona Cowie's Criticism of Nativism. *Mind* 110: 99–148.

—— & PYLYSHYN, Z. (1988). Connectionist and Cognitive Architecture: A Critical Analysis. *Cognition* 28: 3–71.

FODOR, J. D. (1998). Unambiguous Triggers. *Linguistic Inquiry* 29: 1–36.

—— & CROWTHER, C. (in press). Understanding Stimulus Poverty Arguments. *Linguistic Review*, special issue on innateness.

FOX, D., & GRODZINSKY, Y. (1998). Children's Passive: A View from the *By*-Phrase. *Linguistic Inquiry*, 29: 281–92.

FRANCIS, N., & KUČERA, H. (1982). *Frequency Analysis of English Usage: Lexicon and Grammar*. Boston, Mass.: Houghton Mifflin.

FRANK, R., & KAPUR, S. (1996). On the Use of Triggers in Parameter Setting. *Linguistic Inquiry* 27: 623–60.

FREIDIN, R. (1989). Linguistic Theory and Language Acquisition: A Note on Structure-Dependence. *Behavioral and Brain Sciences* 14: 618–19.

GALLISTEL, C. R. (1990). *The Organization of Learning*. Cambridge, Mass.: MIT Press.

GERKEN, L. A. (1991). The Metrical Basis for Children's Subjectless Sentences. *Journal of Memory and Language* 30: 431–51.

GIBSON, E., & WEXLER, K. (1994). Triggers. *Linguistic Inquiry* 25: 355–407.

GILLIS, S., DURIEUX, G., & DAELEMANS, W. (1995). A Computational Model of P&P: Dresher & Kaye (1990) Revisited. In M. Verrips & F. Wijnen (eds.), *Approaches to Parameter Setting*. Amsterdam Series in Child Language Development, 4: 135–73.

GLEITMAN, L. (1981). Maturational Determinants of Language Growth. *Cognition* 10: 115–26.

GOLD, E. M. (1967). Language Identification in the Limit. *Information and Control* 10: 447–74.

GOULD, S. J. (1977). *Ontogeny and Phylogeny*. Cambridge, Mass.: Harvard University Press.

GREENBERG, J. (1963). Some Universals of Grammar with Particular Reference to the Order of Meaningful Elements. In J. Greenberg (ed.), *Universals of Language*. Cambridge, Mass.: MIT Press, 73–113.

GUASTI, M. T. (1992). Verb Syntax in Italian Child Grammar. *Geneva Generative Papers* 1: 115–22.

HAEGEMAN, L. (1995). Root Infinitives, Tense, and Truncated Structures. *Language Acquisition* 4: 205–55.

HALLE, M. (1962). Phonology in Generative Grammar. *Word* 18: 54–72.

—— (1983). On Distinctive Features and Their Articulatory Implementation. *Natural Language and Linguistic Theory* 1: 91–107.

—— (1990). An Approach to Morphology. *Proceedings of the North Eastern Linguistic Society* 20: 150–84.

—— (1997a). Some Consequences of the Representation of Words in Memory. *Lingua* 100: 91–100.

—— (1997b). Distributed Morphology: Impoverishment and Fission. In *PF: Papers at the Interface*. Cambridge, Mass.: MIT Working Papers in Linguistics, 425–50.

—— (1998). The Stress of English Words 1968–1998. *Linguistic Inquiry* 29: 539–68.

—— (2000). Review of Steven Pinker's *Words and Rules: Ingredients of Language*. *Trends in Cognitive Science* 4: 289.

—— & MARANTZ, A. 1993. Distributed Morphology. In K. Hale & S. J. Keyser (eds.) *The View From Building 20*. Cambridge, Mass.: MIT Press, 111–76.

—— & MOHANAN, K.-P. (1985). Segmental Phonology of Modern English. *Linguistic Inquiry*, 16: 57–116.

HALLE, M., & YANG, C. D. (2002). Phonological Rules and the Storage of Words. MS, Massachusetts Institute of Technology and Yale University.

HOCKETT, C. (1968). *The State of the Art*. The Hague: Mouton.

HUANG, C.-H. J. (1984). On the Distribution and Reference of Empty Pronouns. *Linguistic Inquiry* 15: 531–74.

HUBEL, D., & WIESEL, T. (1962). Receptive Fields, Binocular Interaction and Functional Architecture in the Cat's Visual Cortex. *Journal of Physiology* 160: 106–54.

HYAMS, N. (1986). *Language Acquisition and the Theory of Parameters*. Dordrecht: Reidel.

—— (1991). A Reanalysis of Null Subjects in Child Language. In J. Weissenborn, H. Goodluck, & T. Roeper (eds.), *Theoretical Issues in Language Acquisition: Continuity and Change in Development*. Hillsdale, NJ: Erlbaum, 249–67.

—— (1996). The Underspecification of Functional Categories in Early Grammar. In H. Clahsen (ed.), *Generative Perspectives on Language Acquisition*. Amsterdam: John Benjamins, 91–128.

—— & WEXLER, K. (1993). On the Grammatical Basis of Null Subjects in Child Language. *Linguistic Inquiry* 24: 421–59.

JAEGGLI, O., & SAFIR, K. (1989). Introduction. In O. Jaeggli & K. Safir (eds.), *The Null Subject Parameter*. Dordrecht: Kluwer, 1–44.

JAKOBSON, ROMAN. (1941/68). *Child Language, Aphasia and Phonological Universals*. The Hague: Mouton.

JENKINS, L. (1999). *Biolinguistics*. Cambridge: Cambridge University Press.

KAYNE, R. (1975). *French Syntax: The Transformational Cycle*. Cambridge, Mass.: MIT Press.

—— (1991). Romance Clitics, Verb Movement, and PRO. *Linguistic Inquiry* 22: 647–86.

—— (1994). *The Antisymmetry of Syntax*. Cambridge, Mass.: MIT Press.

—— (2000). Microparametric Syntax: Some Introductory Remarks. In R. Kayne, *Parameters and Universals*. Oxford: Oxford University Press, 3–9.

KEENAN, E. (2001). The Historical Creation of Reflexive Pronouns in English. MS, University of California at Los Angeles.

VAN KEMENADE, A. (1987). *Syntactic Case and Morphological Case in the History of English*. Dordrecht: Foris.

KIPARSKY, P. (1973). 'Elsewhere' in Phonology. In S. Anderson & P. Kiparsky (eds.), *A Festschrift for Morris Halle*. New York: Holt, Rinehart, & Winston, 93–106.

—— (1997). The Rise of Positional Licensing. In A. van Kemenade & N. Vincent (eds.), *Parameters of Morphosyntactic Change*. Cambridge: Cambridge University Press, 460–94.

KOHL, K. (1999). An Analysis of Finite Parameter Learning in Linguistic Spaces. Master's thesis. Massachusetts Institute of Technology.

KROCH, A. (1989). Reflexes of Grammar in Patterns of Language Change. *Language Variation and Change* 1: 199–244.

—— (2001). Syntactic Change. In M. Baltin & C. Collins (eds.), *The Handbook of Contemporary Syntactic Theory*. Oxford: Blackwell, 699–729.

—— & TAYLOR, A. (1997). Verb Movement in Old and Middle English: Dialect

Variation and Language Contact. In A. van Kemenade & N. Vincent (eds.), *Parameters of Morphosyntactic Change*. Cambridge: Cambridge University Press, 297–325.

—— —— & RINGE, D. (2000) The Middle English Verb-Second Constraint: A Case Study in Language Contact. In S. Herring, P. van Reneen, & L. Schosler (eds.), *Textual Parameters in Older Languages*. Philadelphia, Penn.: Benjamins, 353–91.

KUHL, P., WILLIAMS, K., LACERDA, F., STEVENS, K., & LINDBLOM, B. (1992). Linguistic Experience Alters Phonetic Perception in Infants by 6 Months of Age. *Science* 255: 606–8.

LABOV, W. (1969). Contraction, Deletion, and Inherent Variability of the English Copula. *Language* 45: 715–62.

LACHTER, J., & BEVER, T. G. (1988). The Relation between Linguistic Structure and Theories of Language Learning: A Constructive Critique of Some Connectionist Learning Models. *Cognition* 28: 195–247.

LEGATE, J. A. (1999). Was the Argument That Was Made Empirical? MS, Massachusetts Institute of Technology.

—— & YANG, C. D. (in press). Empirical Re-Assessments of Stimulus Poverty Arguments. *Linguistic Review*, special issue on innateness.

LEGATE, J. A., & YANG, C. D. (2002). Condition B is Elsewhere. MS, Massachusetts Institute of Technology and Yale University.

LEVINSON, S. (2000). *Presumptive Meanings: The Theory of Generalized Conversational Implicature*. Cambridge, Mass.: MIT Press.

LEVY, Y., & VAINIKKA, A. (1999). The Development of a Mixed Null Subject System: A Cross-linguistic Perspective with Data on the Acquisition of Hebrew. *Language Acquisition* 8: 363–84.

LEWONTIN, R. C. (1983). The Organism as the Subject and Object of Evolution. *Scientia* 118: 65–82.

—— (1996). Population Genetics. In A. Griffith, J. Miller, D. Suzuki, R. Lewontin, & W. Gelbart, *An Introduction to Genetic Analysis*, 6th edn. San Francisco, Calif.: W. H. Freeman, 779–816.

LIGHTFOOT, D. (1979). *The Principles of Diachronic Syntax*. Cambridge: Cambridge University Press.

—— (1991). *How to Set Parameters*. Cambridge, Mass.: MIT Press.

—— (1997). Shifting Triggers and Diachronic Reanalysis. In A. van Kemenade & N. Vincent (eds.), *Parameters of Morphosyntactic Change*. Cambridge: Cambridge University Press, 253–72.

—— (1998). Promises, Promises: General Learning Algorithms. *Mind and Language* 13: 582–7.

—— (1999). *The Development of Language: Acquisition, Change, and Evolution*. Oxford: Blackwell.

LING, C., & MARINOV, M. (1993). Answering the Connectionist Challenge: A

Symbolic Model of Learning the Past Tense of English Verbs. *Cognition* 49: 235–90.

MACKEN, M. (1980). The Child's Lexical Representation: The 'Puzzle–Puddle–Pickle' Evidence. *Journal of Linguistics* 16: 1–17.

—— (1995). Phonological Acquisition. In J. Goldsmith (ed.), *Handbook of Phonological Theory*. Oxford: Blackwell, 671–96.

MACNAMARA, J. (1982). *Names for Things: A Study of Human Learning*. Cambridge, Mass.: MIT Press.

MACWHINNEY, B., & LEINBACH, J. (1991). Implementations Are Not Conceptualizations: Revising the Verb Learning Model. *Cognition* 29: 121–57.

—— & SNOW, C. (1985). The Child Language Data Exchange System. *Journal of Child Language* 12: 271–96.

MARANTZ, A. (1984). *On the Nature of Grammatical Relations*. Cambridge, Mass.: MIT Press.

MARATSOS, M. (2000). More Overregularizations after all: New Data and Discussion on Marcus, Pinker, Ullman, Hollander, Rosen, & Xu. *Journal of Child Language*, 27: 183–212.

MARCUS, G. (1993). Negative Evidence in Language Acquisition. *Cognition* 46: 53–85.

—— (1998). Can Constructivism Save Connectionism? *Cognition* 66: 153–82.

—— BRINKMANN, U., CLAHSEN, H., WIESE, R., & PINKER, S. (1995). German Inflection: The Exception that Proves the Rule. *Cognitive Psychology* 29: 189–256.

—— PINKER, S., ULLMAN, M., HOLLANDER, M., ROSEN, J., & XU, F. (1992). *Overregularization in Language Acquisition*. Stanford, Calif.: Society for Research in Child Development.

—— SANTORINI, B., & MARCHINIKIEWICZ, M. (1993). Building a Large Annotated Corpus of English: The Penn Tree Bank. *Computational Linguistics* 19: 313–30.

MARLER, P. (1991). The Instinct to Learn. In S. Carey & R. Gelman (eds.), *The Epigenesis of Mind: Essays on Biology and Cognition*. Hillsadale, NJ: Erlbaum, 37–66.

MAYNARD SMITH, J. (1989). *Evolutionary Genetics*. Oxford: Oxford University Press.

MAYR, E. (1963). *Animal Species and Evolution*. Cambridge, Mass.: Harvard University Press.

—— (1982). *The Growth of Biological Thought: Diversity, Evolution, and Inheritance*. Cambridge, Mass.: Harvard University Press.

—— (1993). *One Long Argument*. Cambridge, Mass.: Harvard University Press.

—— & PROVINE, W. (1980). *The Evolutionary Synthesis*. Cambridge, Mass.: Harvard University Press.

MOLNAR, R. (2001). 'Generalize and Sift' as a Model of Inflection Acquisition. Master's thesis, Massachusetts Institute of Technology.

MOONEY, R., & CALIFF, M. (1995). Induction of First-Order Decision Lists: Results on Learning the Past Tense of English Verbs. *Journal of Artificial Intelligence Research* 3: 1–24.

MUFWENE, S. (2001). *The Ecology of Language Evolution*. Cambridge: Cambridge University Press.

MYERS, S. (1987). Vowel Shortening in English. *Natural Language and Linguistic Theory* 5: 485–518.

NARENDRA, K., & THATHACHAR, M. (1989). *Learning Automata*. Englewood Cliffs, NJ: Prentice-Hall.

NEWPORT, E., GLEITMAN, L., & GLEITMAN, H. (1977). Mother, I'd Rather Do It Myself. In C. E. Snow & C. A Ferguson (eds.), *Talking to Children: Language Input and Acquisition*. Cambridge: Cambridge University Press, 109–50.

NIYOGI, P., & BERWICK, R. (1995). The Logical Problem of Language Change. MIT Artificial Intelligence Laboratory Memo No. 1516. Cambridge, Mass.

—— —— (1996). A Language Learning Model for Finite Parameter Spaces. *Cognition* 61: 161–93.

NORMAN, F. (1972). *Markov Processes and Learning Models*. New York: Academic Press.

OSHERSON, D., WEINSTEIN, S., & STOB, M. (1984). Learning Theory and Natural Language. *Cognition* 17: 1–28.

—— —— —— (1986). *Systems that Learn*. Cambridge, Mass.: MIT Press.

PAUL, H. (1890/1970). *Principles of the History of Language*. College Park, Md.: McGrath.

PESETSKY, D. (1995). *Zero Syntax: Experiencer and Cascade*. Cambridge, Mass.: MIT Press.

PHILLIPS, C. (1995). Syntax at Age 2: Cross-linguistic Differences. In *MIT Working Papers in Linguistics* 26. Cambridge, Mass.: MITWPL, 325–82.

PIATTELLI-PALMARINI, M. (1989). Evolution, Selection, and Cognition: From 'Learning' to Parameter Setting in Biology and in the Study of Language. *Cognition* 31: 1–44.

PIERCE, A. (1989). On the Emergence of Syntax: A Crosslinguistic Study. PhD dissertation, Massachusetts Institute of Technology.

PINKER, S. (1984). *Language Learnability and Language Development*. Cambridge, Mass.: Harvard University Press.

—— (1995). Why the Child Holded the Baby Rabbit: A Case Study in Language Acquisition. In L. Gleitman & M. Liberman (eds.), *An Invitation to Cognitive Science: Language*. Cambridge, Mass.: MIT Press, 107–33.

—— (1999). *Words and Rules: The Ingredients of Language*. New York: Basic Books.

—— Lebeaux, D., & Frost, A. (1987). Productivity and Constraints in the Acquisition of the Passive. *Cognition* 26: 195–267.

Pinker, S. & Prince, A. (1988). On Language and Connectionism: Analysis of a Parallel Distributed Model of Language Acquisition. *Cognition* 28: 73–193.

—— —— (1994). Regular and Irregular Morphology and the Psychological Status of Rules of Grammar. In S. Lima, R. Corrigan, & G. Iverson (eds.), *The Reality of Linguistic Rules*. Amsterdam: John Benjamins, 321–51.

Pintzuk, S. (1991). Phrase Structure in Competition: Variation and Change in Old English Word Order. Ph.D. dissertation, University of Pennsylvania.

Poeppel, D., & Wexler, K. (1993). The Full Competence Hypothesis. *Language* 69: 1–33.

Pollock, J.-Y. (1989). Verb Movement, Universal Grammar, and the Structure of IP. *Linguistic Inquiry* 20: 365–424.

Prasada, S., & Pinker, S. (1993). Generalization of Regular and Irregular Morphology. *Language and Cognitive Processes* 8: 1–56.

Prossnitz, I. B. A. (1579). Preface to *Sefer Shir Ha-Shirim* (Song of Songs). Cracow.

Pullum, G. (1996). Learnability, Hyperlearning, and the Poverty of the Stimulus. Paper presented at the parasession on learnability, 22nd Annual Meeting of the Berkeley Linguistics Society, Berkeley, Calif.

Quang, Phuc Dong. (1971). English Sentences with Overt Grammatical Subject. In A. Zwicky, P. Salus, R. Binnick, & A. Vanek (eds.), *Studies Out in Left Field: Defamatory Essays Presented to James D. McCawley*. Amsterdam: John Benjamins, 3–10.

Randall, J. (1990). Catapults and Pendulums: The Mechanisms of Language Acquisition. *Linguistics* 28: 1381–406.

Rispoli, M. (1999). Review of Elman et al., *Rethinking Innateness. Journal of Child Language* 26: 217–60.

Rizzi, L. (1986). Null Object in Italian and the Theory of Pro. *Linguistic Inquiry* 17: 501–57.

—— (1994). Some Notes on Linguistic Theory and Language Development: The Case of Root Infinitives. *Language Acquisition* 3: 371–93.

Roberts, I. (1993). *Verbs and Diachronic Syntax: A Comparative History of English and French*. Dordrecht: Kluwer.

Roeper, T. (2000). Universal Bilingualism. *Bilingualism: Language and Cognition* 2: 169–86.

—— & Rohrbacher, B. (1994). Null Subjects in Early Child English and the Theory of Economy of Projection. Technical Report 94–12. Philadelphia: Institute for Research in Cognitive Science, University of Pennsylvania.

Rosch, E. (1978). Principles of Categorization: A Historical View. In E. Rosch & B. Lloyd (eds.), *Cognition and Categorization*. Mahwah, NJ: Erlbaum, 27–48.

RUMELHART, D., & MCCLELLAND, J. (1986). On Learning the Past Tenses of English Verbs: Implicit Rules or Parallel Distributed Processing? In J. McClelland, D. Rumelhart, & PDP Research Group. *Parallel Distributed Processing: Explorations in the Microstructure of Cognition.* Cambridge, Mass.: MIT Press, 216–71.

SAFFRAN, J., ASLIN, R., & NEWPORT, E. (1996). Statistical Learning by 8-Month Old Infants. *Science* 274: 1926–8.

SAKAS, W., & FODOR, J. D. (2001). The Structural Trigger Learner. In S. Bertolo (ed.), *Language Acquisition and Learnability.* Cambridge: Cambridge University Press, 228–300.

SAMPSON, G. (1989). Language Acquisition: Growth or Learning? *Philosophical Papers* 18: 203–40.

SANKOFF, D. (ed.) (1978). *Language Variation: Models and Methods.* New York: Academic Press.

SANO, T., & HYAMS, N. (1994). Agreement, Finiteness, and the Development of Null Arguments. *Proceedings of the North Eastern Linguistic Society* 24: 543–58.

SANTORINI, B. (1992). Variation and Change in Yiddish Subordinate Clause Word Order. *Natural Language and Linguistic Theory* 10: 595–640.

SAYE, T., & CLAHSEN, H. (2002). Words, Rules, and Stems in the Italian Mental Lexicon. In S. Nooteboom, F. Weerman, & F. Wijnen (eds.), *Storage and Computation in the Language Faculty.* Boston, Mass.: Kluwer, 76–108.

SEIDENBERG, M. (1997). Language Acquisition and Use: Learning and Applying Probabilistic Constraints. *Science* 275: 1599–604.

SHLONSKY, U. (1997). *Clause Structure and Word Order in Hebrew and Arabic.* Oxford: Oxford University Press.

SMITH, N. (1973). *The Acquisition of Phonology: A Case Study.* Cambridge: Cambridge University Press.

STAMPE, D. (1979). *A Dissertation on Natural Phonology.* New York: Garland.

STROMSWOLD, K. (1990). Learnability and the Acquisition of Auxiliaries. PhD dissertation, Massachusetts Institute of Technology.

—— & ZIMMERMAN, K. (1999). Acquisition of *Nein* and *Nicht* and the VP-Internal Subject Stage in German. *Language Acquisition* 8: 101–27.

TESAR, B., & SMOLENSKY, P. (2000). *Learnability in Optimality Theory.* Cambridge, Mass.: MIT Press.

THORNTON, R., & WEXLER, K. (1999). *Principle B, VP Ellipsis, and Interpretation in Child Grammar.* Cambridge, Mass.: MIT Press.

TORRENS, V. (1995). The Acquisition of Inflection in Spanish and Catalan. In *MIT Working Papers in Linguistics* 26. Cambridge, Mass.: MITWPL, 434–58.

TRAVIS, L. (1984). Parameters and Effects of Word Order Variation. PhD dissertation, Massachusetts Institute of Technology.

ULLMAN, M., CORKIN, S., PINKER, S., COPPOLA, M., LOCASCIO, J., and GROWDON,

J. H. (1993). Neural Modularity in Language: Evidence from Alzheimer's and Parkinson's Disease. Abstract presented at the 23rd Annual Meeting of the Society for Neuroscience, Washington, DC.

VALIAN, V. (1990). Null Subjects: A Problem for Parameter-Setting Models of Language Acquisition. *Cognition* 35: 105–22.

—— (1991). Syntactic Subjects in the Early Speech of American and Italian Children. *Cognition* 40: 21–82.

WALLER, B. (1997). Against a Metrical Basis for Subject Drop in Child Language. MS, Massachusetts Institute of Technology.

WANG, Q., LILLO-MARTIN, D., BEST, C., & LEVITT, A. (1992). Null Subject vs. Null Object: Some Evidence from the Acquisition of Chinese and English. *Language Acquisition* 2: 221–54.

WEINBERG, A. (1990). Markedness vs. Maturation: The Case of Subject–Auxiliary Inversion. *Language Acquisition* 1: 169–94.

WEINREICH, U., LABOV, W., & HERZOG, M. (1968). Empirical Foundations for a Theory of Language Change. In W. Lehman & Y. Malkiel (eds.), *Directions for Historical Linguistics: A Symposium*. Austin: University of Texas Press, 95–188.

WEVERINK, M. (1989). The Subject in Relation to Inflection in Child Language. MA thesis, University of Utrecht.

WEXLER, K. (1994). Optional Infinitives, Head Movement, and the Economy of Derivation in Child Language. In D. Lightfoot & N. Hornstein (eds.), *Verb Movement*. Cambridge: Cambridge University Press, 305–50.

—— (1998). Very Early Parameter Setting and the Unique Checking Constraint: A New Explanation of the Optional Infinitive Stage. *Lingua* 106: 23–79.

—— & CULICOVER, P. (1980). *Formal Principles of Language Acquisition*. Cambridge, Mass.: MIT Press.

WIJNEN, F. (1999). Verb Placement in Dutch Child Language: A Longitudinal Analysis. MS, University of Utrecht.

XU, F., & PINKER, S. (1995). Weird Past Tense Forms. *Journal of Child Language* 22: 531–56.

YANG, C. D. (1996). Psychological Reality, Type Transparency, and Minimalist Sentence Processing. MS, Massachusetts Institute of Technology.

—— (1999). Two Grammars Are Better than One. *Bilingualism: Language and Cognition* 2: 201–3.

—— (2000). Dig–Dug, Think–Thunk. Review of Steven Pinker's *Words and Rules*. *London Review Of Books* 22 (16).

—— (2002). Panda's Thumbs and Irregular Verbs. MS, Yale University.

—— (in press) Parametric Learning and Parsing. In R. Berwick (ed.), *Principle-Based Parsing II: From Theory to Practice*. Boston, Mass.: Kluwer.

—— & GUTMANN, S. (1999). Language Learning via Martingales. Paper presented at the 6th Conference of the Mathematics of Language, Orlando, Fla.

YIP, K., and SUSSMAN, G. (1996). A Computational Model for the Acquisition and Use of Phonological Knowledge. Cambridge, Mass.: MIT Artificial Intelligence Laboratory, Memo 1575.

—— —— (1997). Sparse Representations for Fast, One-Shot Learning. Paper presented at the National Conference on Artificial Intelligence, Orlando, Fla.

# Index of Authors

Allen, S. 11 n.
Andersen, H. 125
Atkinson, R. 29

Bailey, C. J. 131–2
Baker, M. 37, 87
Barto, A. 32
Bates, E. 15, 16, 118, 137
Battye, A. 125
Behrens, H. 22
Berko, J. 59–60
Bertolo, S. 42 n.
Berwick, R. 17, 18, 19 n., 20, 28, 45 n., 54, 132
Bever, T. 60
Bloom, P. 22, 54, 103, 120
Bloomfield, L. 128
Borer, H. 10, 11 n.
Boser, K. 103
de Boysson-Bardies, B. 53
Bromberg, H. 10, 122 n.
Brown, R. 22, 73, 104
Bush, R. 29, 30
Bybee, J. 85

Califf, M. 68
Caselli, M. 118, 137
Changeux, J. P. 151
Charniak, E. 148 n.
Chomsky, N. 1, 2, 3, 4, 5 n., 7, 9, 18, 40 n., 54, 62, 64, 85, 114 n., 115 n., 125, 151
Church, K. 42 n.
Clahsen, H. 67, 69 n., 109, 118
Clark, E. 68 n., 83
Clark, R. 19, 28 n., 34–5, 37, 54, 132–3
Cowie, F. 109
Crain, S. 2, 3 n., 11 n., 111
Crowther, C. 17
Culicover, P. 17, 28, 73

Demuth, K. 11 n.
Deprez, V. 106–7
Dresher, E. 17–18, 41, 42

Edelman, G. 151
Edmonds, J. 40
Elman, J. 15, 16
Embick, D. 59

Fassi-Fehri, A. 35, 105
Felix, S. 10
Fisher, C. 112–13 n.
Fodor, J. A. 8, 60, 85, 145
Fodor, J. D. 11, 17, 19, 34, 41, 51 n., 146 n.
Fox, D. 8 n.
Frank, R. 18
Frazier, L. 146 n.
Freidin, R. 109

Gerken, L. A. 22
Gibson, E. 17, 18, 48, 55
Gillis, S. 42 n.
Gleitman, L. 10
Gold, M. 5, 45
Gould, S. J. 101
Greenberg, J. 35
Grodzinksy, Y. 11 n.
Guasti, M. 67, 93, 118
Gutmann, S. 29 n., 44

Haegeman, L. 85, 103, 106, 123
Halle, M. 9, 59, 62–4, 68, 82, 85, 97, 125
Hanlon, C. 73
Hockett, C. 128
Hornstein, N. 119 n.
Huang, J. 115, 149
Hubel, D. 151
Hyams, N. 10, 17, 21, 103, 122, 149

## Index of Authors

Jaeggli, O. 104, 149
Jakobson, R. 9, 53
Jenkins, L. 2

Kapur, S. 18
Kaye, J. 17, 41
Kayne, R. 37, 147
van Kemenade, A. 138–9
Kiparsky, P. 70, 139
Kohl, K. 18, 56
Kroch, A. 131–2, 133, 138–9
Kuhl, P. 53

Labov, W. 33
Lachter, J. 60
Legate, J. A. 3 n., 102 n., 113, 146
Leinbach, J. 68
Lenneberg, E. 1
Levy, Y. 67, 118
Lewontin, R. 9 n., 15, 25
Lightfoot, D. 17, 31, 35 n., 41, 53, 57, 125, 135
Ling, C. 68

MacWhinney, B. 7, 68, 77, 112, 117 n., 120
McClelland, J. 16, 59–60
McNamara, J. 8, 9, 22
Macken, M. 53, 83
Marantz, A. 59, 62, 65 n.
Maratsos, M. 90 n.
Marcus, G. 10, 16, 60–2, 69, 73, 77, 82, 89, 92, 98
Marcus, M. 135
Marinov, M. 68
Marler, P. 151
Maynard Smith, J. 9 n.
Mayr, E. 8, 24
Moder, C. 85
Mohanan, K. 62, 97
Molnar, R. 68
Mooney, R. 68
Mosteller, F. 29, 30
Mufwene, S. 143
Muller, H. J. 14
Myers, S. 64 n., 65, 82

Nakayama, M. 2, 111
Narendra, K. 32
Newport, E. 30
Niyogi, P. 18, 19 n., 20, 45 n., 132
Norman, F. 32

Osherson, D. 19

Paul, H. 125
Penke, M. 67, 118
Phillips, C. 21 n., 23, 67, 118, 123 n.
Piattelli-Palmarini, M. 53
Pierce, A. 7, 103, 106–7, 108
Pinker, S. 9, 10, 11 n., 16, 22, 54, 59–61, 67–9, 73–5, 85–95
Pintzuk, S. 133, 138–9
Poeppel, D. 103, 107–8
Pollock, J.-Y. 40
Prasada, S. 16, 60, 87
Prince, A. 60, 69 n., 76, 85, 87, 97
Provine, W. 8
Pullum, G. 3 n., 102, 109–12
Pylyshyn, Z. 8, 60

Quang, P. D. 59

Randall, J. 19
Rispoli, M. 16
Rizzi, L. 8, 17, 115, 122
Roberts, I. 19, 34–5, 125, 132–3, 134–7
Roeper, T. 10, 54, 122 n.
Rohrbacher, B. 10, 122 n.
Rosch, E. 85
Rothweiler, M. 69 n.
Rumelhart, D. 16, 59–60

Saffran, J. 16
Safir, K. 104, 149
Sakas, W. 20, 51 n.
Sampson, G. 3 n., 102, 109, 112 n.
Sankoff, D. 33
Sano, T. 122
Santorini, B. 133
Saye, T. 69 n.
Seidenberg, M. 15
Shlonsky, U. 35, 105–6

Slobin, D. 85
Smith, N. 83
Smolensky, P. 41 n.
Snow, C. 7, 34, 43, 57, 68, 77, 104, 112, 117 n., 120
Sonderegger, M. 49
Stampe, D. 53
Stromswold, K. 106–7, 148
Sussman, G. 68, 93, 143
Sutton, R. 32

Taylor, A. 133, 138–9
Tesar, B. 41 n.
Thatharchar, M. 32
Tokura, H. 112–13 n.
Torrens, V. 118
Travis, L. 40 n.

Ullman, M. 95

Vainikka, A. 67, 118

Valian, V. 8, 19–20, 22, 40, 103–4, 111, 118, 120
Vance, B. 136

Waller, B. 122 n.
Wang, Q. 21, 103, 117, 119–20, 121
Weinberg, A. 54
Weinrich, U. 20, 131–2
Weverink, M. 8, 92
Wexler, K. 7, 8, 10, 11 n., 17–18, 28, 48, 55, 73, 93, 103, 107–8, 122
Wiesel, T. 151
Wijnen, F. 107

Xu, F. 60, 67, 69, 86, 87 n.

Yang, C. D. 3 n., 29 n., 41, 44, 54, 59, 68, 89, 96, 102 n., 143, 146
Yip, K. 66, 93, 143

Zimmerman, K. 106–7

# Subject Index

acquisition model
  abstract 4–5, 19, 145
  necessity of quantitativeness 6, 9
  need for concrete mechanisms 5, 101–2
  parsimony 10
analogy 83–4
  historical change 87–9
  misirregularization 86, 87
  other languages 86
  rhyme 84
  weak force 85–6
  vagueness of formulation 83, 84

biolinguistics 2–4, 150
Blocking Principle 60–1
  Absolute 62, 73
  innateness 73–4
  learning 74, 74 n.
  Stochastic 73

CHILDES database 7, 34, 43, 57, 68, 77, 104, 112, 117 n., 120
competing grammars:
  case systems 54
  Chinese vs. English and Italian 117–18
  English vs. Chinese 118–19
  English vs. Italian 118
  Italian vs. English and Chinese 117–18
  phonology learning 53
  verb initial and verb second 105–9
  see also verb second
Continuity Hypothesis 9–10, 22
cue-based learning 18, 39, 41–2, 42 n.

Darwinian evolution 24
  population thinking 25
  variational thinking 25
developmental compatibility 6–9

empiricist statistical learning 8–9, 14–19
  and past tense 16, 60
  connectionism 60
  disparities between children and adults 7–9, 11
  empirical coverage 15–16
  probabilistic grammars 148–9
  see also Wug-test
explanatory continuity 9–12

genetic algorithm 28 n., 54–5

innateness 2, 7, 14, 109–10, 125–6, 148, 150

language acquisition:
  domain specificity and neutrality 145–8
  imperfection in child language 23–4, 54
  linguistic theories 146–50
  maturation 10–11
  see also language growth
language change:
  compared to biological evolution 127, 129, 144
  contingency and predictability 129, 143–4
  input to acquisition 127–8, 133
  language acquisition 126
  mis-learning as cause 128
  population phenomenon 128
  sociological factors 129
  Universal Grammar 125
  see also variational change
language development:
  comparative 102–3, 108, 111, 116, 118–19
  gradualness 23, 27
  input frequency 6–8, 109–14, 116–17, 119
  see also subject drop, verb raising, verb second

## Subject Index

language growth:
  in other species 151
  neurological evidence 151
  variational model 151
language variation 20, 32–3, 151
  intrinsic 53–4, 150
  linguistic theory 3–4, 25, 150
learnability 5, 45
  formal sufficiency 5–6
  language change 6
  sample complexity 45–6

misirregularization 60
  as analogy 86–7
  compared to agreement acquisition 67
  rarity of 67, 69, 86, 87 n.
  word-rule association 69

naive parameter learner 43–8
  computational cost 37
  definition 43–4
  grammar fitness distribution 43, 46–8, 55–8
  Hamming distance 47
  interference in learning 36–9, 41–2, 45, 53
  learning rate 48–53
  sample complexity 45–6
  with batch 49–50

optional infinitives (OI) 8
  competence deficits 23
  null subjects 122–3
  past tense 92–3
overregularization 60
  default rule 61–2, 92–3
  see also Rules and Competition

parameter 4, 26, 126, 147
  interference 36–9
  signature 39–41
  see also naive parameter learner
past tense acquisition 59–97
  child performance 77–83, 89–94, 98–100
  default rule 61, 66–70, 92–3

economy of word storage 63–4, 68
  individual variation 76, 79, 90
  language acquisition 67–8, 92–3
  longitudinal trends 91–3
  phonological theory 62–4, 143
  role of memory 61–2, 66, 95
  sound change 88–9, 95–6
  vowel shortening 66
performance 10
  explanation of errors 11, 97, 108–9
  null subjects 10–11, 119–20, 121 n.
population genetics 9, 133

Rules and Competition 61, 71
  difference with Words and Rule 63–4
  free-rider effect 80–2, 86
  induction of rules 68, 92–3
  learning algorithm 71–2
  partial regularity 87–9, 96
  predictions 72
  rule-based phonology 7–8, 97, 149–50
  rules for irregular verbs 64–5, 97–8
  vowel shortening 66, 82–3
  word-rule association 64–6, 68–9
  see also Blocking Principle

Structural Triggering Learner 19, 41–3, 41 n.
structure dependency 2–3, 109–13
  see also innateness
subject drop 7–8, 10–11, 21, 23, 104, 111, 114–23
  Avoid Pronoun Principle 119 n.
  expletive as signature 40, 103–4, 111, 114, 119
  pro-drop and morphology 114–51, 119
  topicalization 115
  triggering 20–2
  vs. object drop 115, 117, 120–1

transformational learning 15, 17, 20, 42
triggering 12
  ambiguous input 19–20
  developmental problems 20–2
  early parameter setting hypothesis 23, 107–8, 121–2

failure to converge 19–20
noisy input 19–20
and subject drop 21
*see also* transformational learning

variational change 129–31
advantage of grammar 130
*see also* penalty probability
formal model 130–2
fundamental theorem 131
limits of model 150
S-shape curve 131–2
transient multiple grammars 133
variational model 26–30
developmental rate 33–4
formal model 30–2
general learning 24, 28–9
linguistic theories 147, 149
penalty probability 31, 130
psychological plausibility 28, 37
*see also* naive parameter learner
stable multiple grammars 32–4, 133
strong generative capacity 28, 119
with unambiguous input 34–6
*see also* language change, language development
verb raising 6–7, 40
early acquisition 7
signature 40, 103, 104

verb second (V2):
acquisition 35, 105–9
against early setting 107
compared to subject drop 108
effective signature 105
lack of unambiguous evidence 34–6

Verb Second change:
advantage over SVO grammar 135–6
dialectal variations in Old English 139–42
and language contact 141–3
interacting with pro-drop 135–6
Old English 138–42
Old French 134–7
residual V2 139–40, 141
Romance languages 137
stability of 95, 134, 142–3

Wh-movement 40, 104, 120, 148
Words and Rule 60–1, 89, 97
associative memory 61
centrality of frequency 60–1, 75–6, 76 n.
default rule 60, 92–3
difference with Rules and Competition 63
failure of frequency 79, 83, 89–90, 91–92
mechanisms 75–6, 85
*Wug*-test 59–60